A Glad Beginning—A Gracious Ending

A GLAD BEGINNING- A GRACIOUS ENDING

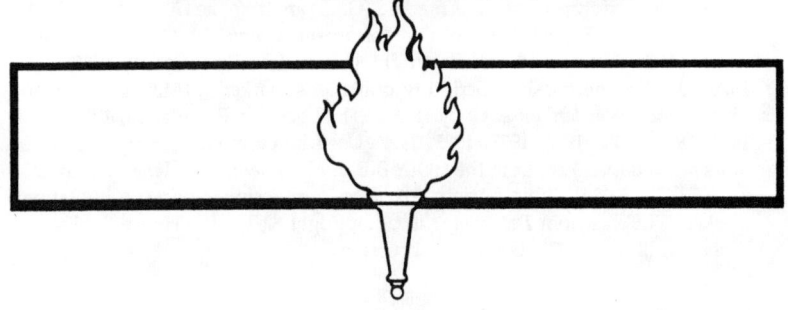

D. L. Lowrie

BROADMAN PRESS
Nashville, Tennessee

© Copyright 1988 • Broadman Press
All rights reserved
4225-48
ISBN: 0-8054-2548-9
Dewey Decimal Classification: 253
Subject Heading: MINISTRIES // MINISTRY
Library of Congress Catalog Card Number: 88:5023
Printed in the United States of America

Unless otherwise indicated, Scripture quotations are from the King James Version of the Bible. Scripture quotations marked (GNB) are from the *Good News Bible*, the Bible in Today's English Version. Old Testament: Copyright © American Bible Society 1976; New Testament: Copyright © American Bible Society 1966, 1971, 1976. Used by permission. Scripture quotations marked (NASB) are from the *New American Standard Bible*. Copyright © The Lockman Foundation, 1960, 1962, 1963, 1968, 1971, 1972, 1973, 1975, 1977. Used by permission. Scripture quotations marked (NIV) are from the HOLY BIBLE *New International Version*, copyright © 1978, New York Bible Society. Used by permission. Scripture quotations marked (TLB) are from *The Living Bible*. Copyright © Tyndale House Publishers, Wheaton, Illinois, 1971. Used by permission.

Library of Congress Cataloging-in-Publication Data

Lowrie, D. L., 1935-
  A glad beginning, a gracious ending.

  (Broadman leadership series)
  1. Clergy—Appointment, call, and election.
I. Title. II. Series.
BV4012.L68 1988   253'.2   88-5023
ISBN 0-8054-2548-9

To
Alice
a faithful companion through all the changes of life

Contents

Introduction   9
  Part I: Glad Beginnings
  1. A Conviction: The Right Move   15
  2. A Partnership: What the Church Can Do   22
  3. An Appreciation: A Look at the Past   28
  4. An Acceptance: A Spiritual Marriage   34
  5. An Understanding: An Agreement About Ministry   41
  6. A Vision: Establishing Some Goals   49
  7. A Plan: Staying with the Basics   55
  Part II: Gracious Endings
  8. Leadership: Signs You Should Move   65
  9. Openness: Sharing Your Heart   73
10. Gratitude: Saying Your "Thank-You's"   79
11. Preparation: Making It Easy for Your Successor   85
12. Business: Leave Your House in Order   92
13. Ethics: Relating to your Successor in a Christian Way   98
14. The Parting: What the Church Can Do   104

Introduction

This book is a sincere attempt to meet an obvious and felt need. After having changed pastorates seven times in my years of ministry, and having blundered my way through them without much mature guidance, I began to reflect on these experiences. I asked myself some questions. What have I learned? What could I have done differently? What mistakes have I made or observed? This book is the result of that prayerful reflection.

Though I searched for ideas in a score of places, this book is not the result of research. Little has been written on the subject of beginning and ending pastorates. I have questioned others to see if their experiences were similar to mine.

You need to know the basic assumptions that I have made. I have assumed that a person is in the pastoral ministry as the result of a divine call. Such a summons from the Lord thrust me into the ministry in my late teen years. This call has sustained me through the times of testing. The God revealed in Holy Scripture is the God who calls and sends. He called and sent Abraham. He sent the prophets. He sent His Son. He sent the twelve. He sent Saul of Tarsus. He continues to call and send.

I also have assumed that the true Bishop, the Lord Jesus, directs a particular person to a particular place of ministry. While this assumption will be debated by some, it has been a foundational principle on which I have built my life. This puts the ministry under the lordship of Christ in a special way. If this assumption is valid, the pastor and the church must approach a pastoral change with a prayerful attitude. This may complicate the decision-making process about a change since it is more than a professional change.

Another assumption is that even a servant of the Lord can do things that will favorably affect the course of his ministry. Being a servant of the Lord does not make you a robot. God grants a remarkable degree of freedom to the pastor as to the form his ministry will take. He is free to form his ministry to fit his spiritual gifts, abilities, and the unique circumstances in which he finds himself. He is not free to change his message, but he can adapt the methods he uses. The pastoral letters of Paul support this idea. While they give helpful counsel to the pastor, they do not spell out the "how to" of the pastoral ministry. We must give form to the ministry. We can surely learn how to do this, and we can develop skills in which to do this.

I have assumed also that the pastor has the major part to play in the successful beginning of a pastorate and its gracious ending. While he cannot do it alone, it will not happen unless he does the right things in the right spirit. I have addressed some very practical words to the church in these chapters, but I have deliberately placed the heavier burden on the pastor. In most cases he will find a responsive church if he takes the right initiative. So these chapters are addressed primarily to the shepherd of the sheep.

I have made one other assumption: How you begin and end is important! How you end your present pastorate will affect the beginning for your successor and may impact the church for several years to come. How you begin a new pastorate will affect profoundly your ability to do the work of God among the people. I want to weep when I remember

Introduction

the way the possibility of a good work has been destroyed by a flawed beginning by men I have known. While they sought to blame others, they were responsible. If they had followed some of the practical steps set forth in this book, their whole ministry would have followed a more fruitful path.

Though this book is written from the perspective of the pastor, many of the principles are applicable to any member of the ministerial staff. How you begin and end is also important for you personally and for the congregation.

This book does not pretend to be an exhaustive treatment of the subject. Some things suggested may not fit your personality or spiritual gifts, but they will provide you an outline around which you can form your own plan of action.

The book is divided into two parts. This results in some duplication of ideas, but it will make it easier to use as a practical handbook as you live through these experiences.

Part I
A Glad Beginning

1
A Conviction
The Right Move

So you are the pastor of a church that governs itself congregationally! While this provides many blessings to your pastoral calling, it adds a heavy responsibility to your life. You must make the decision concerning where you will serve. You will have the last word in the decision as to whether you will accept the invitation to become pastor of the church. While you do it with an awareness that the ultimate word is spoken by God in such a situation, it is not always easy to know what God is saying.

How can I be sure that this is the right move for me and my family? This question has caused many sleepless nights for the dedicated pastor. While you know that you are a "man of God," under a divine summons to serve Him in the ministry, you also know that you are a man of flesh, a man in this world. When decision-making time comes, you have difficulty escaping worldly influences and just thinking and deciding as a man of God. Many times you are very comfortable where you are when you are confronted with a decision. How much value do you place on your comfort in such a decision? Many times the decision comes when you are rather unhappy where you are. Could your desire to move be nothing more than a desire to escape a difficult situation? What if the Chief Shepherd had chosen the path of least difficulty?

While nothing can take the agony out of such decisions, some things have been helpful to pastors through the years. They are worthy of consideration.

An Inner Peace

You are a very complex being. You become painfully aware of this complexity when trying to make decisions. A part of the complexity of your being is the subjective or spiritual side. It is a part of your being that you have difficulty explaining to others. Yet, the subjective must be considered when you are making a decision.

What do you look for subjectively? You should look for an inner peace about the decision. A word from the apostle Paul can be helpful. He wrote, "Let the peace of Christ rule in your hearts, to which indeed you were called in one body; and be thankful" (Col. 3:15, NASB). The "peace of Christ" is the inner, subjective sense of well-being that comes from a right relationship with God through Christ. The *Good News Bible* translates this admonition, "The peace that Christ gives is to guide you in the decisions that you make." While in the context Paul had in mind decisions relating to your relationship to the body of Christ, the verse has a broader application. To allow this "peace" to rule in your heart is to refrain from anything that destroys this inner peace.

Many get nervous about introducing the subjective into a decision-making process. But if you take seriously the presence of the indwelling Christ, this surely seems like a possibility. Can not the indwelling Christ communicate with our inner spirit through the Holy Spirit? Can He not provide guidance to His servants in this way? The testimony of His people through the years is that He can. He does not usually do it in some mystical sort of way, but rather by just giving an inner sense of peace about the decision you are considering. It is difficult to explain to another person, but you know

A Conviction

in the depth of your inner being that there seems to be a rightness about the decision.

This subjective side is not to be taken as infallible. It needs to be kept in balance with the other considerations. It will, however, make it easier to have a good beginning if you make your move with this inner peace.

An Outward Providence

Outward providence is also open to subjective interpretation. Some outward circumstantial things can be sources of assurance that you have made the right move. At least two have helped decision makers who want to be in the will of God.

You can be assured by *providential timing*. In the ways of God in the life of man, timing is always an important factor. In the biblical account of Abraham's life, Sarah gave birth to Isaac at the "set time." (Gen. 21:2) The philosopher of the Bible declared, "To every thing there is a season, and a time to every purpose under the heaven" (Eccl. 3:1). Even though the extended list does not include "a time to stay, and a time to move," I want to consider it.

Providential timing will be right for the congregation you have been serving. You should assume that the change would not be hurtful to the congregation you are to leave. This does not mean that it should not cause them grief. All of your moves will involve some grief in the church you are leaving. Rather, it means that it will not be hurtful to the ministry of the church. You can always look for the right timing in the decision.

No matter how attractive the invitation might appear to me personally, I have always assumed that I should not make the change if it left my present congregation in a precarious position. Surely if the Lord has led in the launching of a major building program, I, as pastor, should be very cautious about a move before the project is finished. The timing would seem to be off. If I have led the church into a major undertaking of any kind, I should be cautious about abandoning them before it is finished. If I am to have a good beginning in the next assignment, I need to feel right about the time of the move.

The providential timing will be right for your personal ministry. As you look back over your life, you should be able to see a divine pattern developing. Paul made this a sign of sonship in the family of God: "For as many as are led by the Spirit of God, they are the sons of God" (Rom. 8:14). It is easy to see how God had providentially prepared His servants in the Bible. He sent Moses to the back side of the desert for forty years to get him ready to lead His people out of Egypt. You should anticipate that God has been providentially at work in your past to get you ready for present and future service.

How do you apply this in decision making? Ask yourself, *Does where God has led me in the past seem to have been preparing me for this place?* If the church is facing a major building program, and you have had the joy of leading a church in such a program, could this be considered providential preparation? You must at least consider the possibility.

One church was in a terrible financial condition. A previous pastor had led them to overextend themselves financially. They needed a pastor with money management skills as well as spiritual leadership abilities. He would have to be able to restore the confidence of the laity of the church in the business part of church life. When they approached a pastor who excelled in this area, he wisely considered it providential direction. Several years of fruitful ministry confirmed the rightness of the decision.

Does there seem to be a match between your strengths

and experience and the needs of the congregation? This could be providential timing in your life. This could be a part of the foundation for a glad beginning.

An Exciting Challenge

An exciting challenge is an important element in pastoral ministry. God so created us that we accomplish more when we are excited about what we are doing. Life takes on a new excitement when we are facing challenge.

The church does not necessarily have to be larger to be a challenge. The Lord can cause you to be filled with excitement about a work that is smaller than where you are presently serving. One friend moved from a large, secure, inner-city church to a small, new-mission congregation. He found the challenge of his life in developing a new church rather than in trying to maintain an old one.

The challenge comes from the Lord. He can open your eyes to see potential where others may see only problems. I followed a pastor who had a long and successful ministry at an inner-city church. None of my friends could see a challenge there for me. They saw the problem of maintaining a work in a transitional neighborhood. But, as I prayed about it, the Lord made each of the problems a challenge to me. He does this as He prepares you for the new work. He will show you the "open door" (1 Cor. 16:9, TLB). This becomes a part of the inner conviction that you need to have a good beginning.

A Willing Partner

A move to a new pastorate puts stress on the pastor's family. Your partner in marriage and your children may feel the stress more than you do. Your wife will often have deeper emotional ties to friends than you do. Your children may be at a stage in life that makes a move emotionally devastating. A wise pastor will consider the welfare of his family when considering a move.

A glad beginning is impossible with a bitter, rebellious family. Such a situation usually can be avoided if you include them in the decision-making process. Your partner should be included in the discussion with the search committee. She should accompany you on any visits you make to the prospective church. The children should be taken into your confidence as you work your way through the decision. The ages and maturity of your children will determine how much you share with them and at what point in the decision-making process you share. The whole family should share the prayer time as you seek the will of God. They should feel that their needs are being considered in the decision.

Since the Lord blessed our family with four sons, we have had some experience with this. Looking back upon the moves that we have made, it is easy to see that they ultimately have been good for our children. Even though at the time they were painful for our family, the changes have brought about growth in the personal life of each family member. God has used these experiences to prepare them for the places of service that He has for them.

Seeing a decision become a family decision is a beautiful experience. While you may have the last word, your beginning with the new church will be happier if your family gives their amen to your word.

Confirming Counsel

While looking to the Lord for direction, listen to wise counselors. The wise man in Proverbs observed, "Where no counsel is, the people fall: but in the multitude of counsellors there is safety" (Prov. 11:14).

You need such wise counsel. You need to subject your reasoning and inner thoughts to another. You are capable of having serious blind spots. You may be overlooking an obvious problem. Such counsel may save you from needless pain. However, you may still make the same decision, but you will make it with better understanding. After wise counsel that he should not go to Jerusalem, Paul still felt it was the will of God. But he was better prepared for the crises that developed there (Acts 21).

You probably have access to such counsel. You may be blessed with godly parents who can be helpful. A trusted friend, a denominational worker, another godly pastor, a seminary professor, or even a professional counselor will do. You may want the counsel of one or more of them. You need them to be lovingly honest with you. You will make a more confident decision after such counsel.

If you can begin your new pastorate with a conviction that this is the right place for you at this particular time in your life, you will be on the way to a glad beginning.

2
A Partnership
What the Church Can Do

If the pastor is to have a good beginning, the church must have a part. A successful ministry is never a solo. As a pastor prepares to move his family to the new place of service, he could suggest to the search committee and to the church some things to do to give their ministry together a glad beginning. He should not wait for them to figure out how they can be helpful. This may be the first time many of them have ever welcomed a new pastor.

A Packet About the Community

In most cases you are moving to a new community. A packet of material about the community will help you become acquainted with your new home. The packet could include materials that are provided by the Chamber of Commerce or Visitor's Bureau in most larger communities. It could include a map to the city and anything else that will help a person know more about the community. It might even include a history of the city or a work of fiction that would give you a feel for the area.

This packet could be put together by a member of the search committee. The more at home the pastor and his family feel in their new place of service, the better their beginning will be.

A Task Force

Moving is hard work. It is especially hard on the pastor's wife. A task force of women who are willing to get their hands dirty can be helpful. They can help the wife unpack boxes, put things on shelves, and do the kind of things necessary to get a house ready to be a home. They can care for smaller children. They can make sure there are plenty of hangers for clothes. They can provide meals so the wife does not have to cook for the first day or two. They can make her and the children feel that they are really welcome in their new home.

A word of warning should be given to whomever puts this task force together. Some persons in a congregation should not be on such a committee. Persons who do not believe that the pastor's family should be human should not be on such a task force. The snoopy person, whose main interest might be in some shortcoming of the pastor, should not be on the task force. It is not really the business of others how much or how little furniture the pastor may have. It is not a matter to be discussed at missions meetings that the pastor's wife has a room full of silver.

But a well-chosen task force could make the pastor's wife feel that she has the wisest husband in the world to accept such a church.

A Ready House

Whether you are to live in a parsonage or in your own home (I hope it will be your own home.), getting a house ready to live in is a chore. When the pastor's family arrives and finds the house in readiness, a giant step has been taken toward a glad beginning.

Getting the house ready would include cleaning, yard work, little repairs, and having the telephone, water, and electricity turned on. I still can remember a surgeon who cleaned a yard before we moved in; another time a businessman made sure everything was ready by assigning one of his workmen the task.

This part of the partnership is even more important if the family is moving into a parsonage. However, you should urge the committee not to make any basic changes in the colors or decor of the house without giving your wife a chance to have some input. Most pastor's wives could write a book about some of the juggling they have had to do in attempting to make their furniture match the carpet and paint the church put in the parsonage without consulting with them. When a pastor's wife encounters this, it will be hard to get any gladness into this beginning.

An Emergency List

Emergencies never seem to come at the right time. Have you ever been in a strange situation when one occurred and you did not know who to call or where to turn? This can happen to a pastor's family. It will be of some comfort to the family if they are provided an emergency list when they arrive.

What should be included on the list? The list should include the name of a doctor and his phone number, the name and phone numbers of a good pharmacist, the police phone number, the fire department number, the name and phone number of the chairman of the deacons, and other church leaders the pastor might need to call. Include any other name or number that the pastor or his family might need in an emergency.

Little things like this list convey a big welcome to the new family.

A Reception

While a reception is a poor place to learn the names of the new congregation, it is a wonderful place to feel the acceptance of your new people. It does not have to be an elaborate affair, but it does need to be well planned. It should be something to which the whole congregation is invited. It should include the pastor's whole family. They need to feel that they are being received too. It should include persons from the community who want to help welcome the new pastor.

Some churches have found a way of adding a little spice to the reception. They give the new pastor a food shower. While the history of this kind of event goes back to the days when the church did not provide adequate compensation and this was a supplement, it can still be meaningful to the pastor's family. Each church family brings a food item they feel the pastor's family would need or enjoy. I still remember the time when we received a three-year supply of sugar!

A Guide

The first days of the new pastor's work can be greatly enhanced if he has a guide available. This is the kind of task that a deacon who is retired can do beautifully. He can guide the new pastor to the bank to open an account. He might even introduce him to some of the officers of the bank. He can accompany the pastor on his hospital visits. Hospitals can be threatening places to a stranger. The guide can introduce the new pastor to some shut-ins as they visit together. He can help the new pastor become acquainted with the city as they visit prospects.

This may require more than one person. When done properly, the new pastor will be on his way to a glad beginning.

Financial Assistance

You may be reluctant to discuss financial assistance with the search committee and church, but it is important. You already know that changing churches is an expensive venture. Even though you may receive a larger salary, it will take a while to recoup from the expense of the move.

What can the church do to make this easier on the new pastor? They can at least cover the basic moving costs. Whenever possible, a professional moving company should be used. Moving household goods without damaging them requires professional hands. Even when you have good professionals doing the moving, there may be damage and loss. The church should at least provide the best.

Our church supplements this. We realize that other costs are associated with the move. The day a person arrives we present him with a check equaling one month's salary. That is not his salary for the first month, but is rather a gift to help cover special moving costs. Some such supplement is almost essential today.

The church may need to consider special help in securing housing. A number of churches have found it wise to provide the new pastor with an interest-free loan for a down payment on a house, if he needs it. This money can either be repaid on a monthly basis or paid back whenever the pastor or staff person sells the house. Without such help, some pastors will find themselves with inadequate housing for their family.

The church may also need to consider helping with a house payment on an unsold house in the city from which the new pastor came. In the corporate world, a common practice is for the company to buy the house of the person they are transferring, or hiring, at its appraised value. A church probably would not want to do this, but it can help with the payments until the house is sold. One church makes the payments fully for three months and then considers further help if it is needed.

How important are these things? Very important! It is difficult for the new pastor to have a glad beginning if he is under financial stress created by the change of churches. It is difficult for the pastor's family to be glad about their new home if they have had to move into less-than-adequate housing.

Good Publicity

Every pastor likes to see his picture in the paper. If the Sunday paper arrives with a well-written story about him and the church, he will go to church the first Sunday with a good feeling about the church. In many communities publicity will also be carried by the local radio and television stations. Even the secular media in many communities recognizes that the calling of a new pastor is a worthy news item.

Most of these are things that the church or its representatives must do. Some of them are expensive, but most will cost little. The list is not complete, but it does serve as a reminder that the pastor needs a good partner if he is to have a glad beginning in the new place. Others must assume some responsibility for making good things happen.

3
An Appreciation
A Look at the Past

Every church has a history. It may be entirely oral history, but a story is there. The more aware you become of this history, the better prepared you will be to lead them as pastor. One of your first tasks should be to become acquainted with your new church's history and to develop an appreciation of its past. This will require some study, as well as some carefully guided conversations.

How Do You Look at the Past?

You can look at the past through reading. If you are going to an older congregation, you can probably find a written history of the church. Perhaps a major historical work has been done. When I went to one congregation as pastor, I discovered that Robert Baker, the well-known church historian, had just completed a history of the first one hundred years of the church. He had been commissioned by the congregation to write the history. But a history may be as brief as a few mimeographed pages. You need to become acquainted with it. As you read the history, you will gain an appreciation of the people you are called to serve.

The church may have a collection of historical materials. You may have to do some research and some searching to find the collection since churches are not generally very good stewards of their histories. The collection may contain newspaper clippings about important events. It may be a volume of the Sunday bulletins that has been preserved. It may be volumes of the weekly mailout sent to the church family. A few hours spent browsing through these will enlarge your appreciation of where the congregation has been.

If the church has not been very good at preserving a record of its life, you may be able to borrow some minutes of the local denominational office. It will at least give you some appreciation for the numerical patterns of the church. This may raise some questions you can ask when conversing with longtime leaders of the church. Why was there such dramatic growth in 1954? What happened in 1967 to cause the significant drop in Sunday School attendance? Why did the church baptize so many in 1957? These kinds of questions will uncover a lot of history.

Do you really want to know what has been going on in the life of the church? Spend a day reading the minutes from the deacons' meetings and from the church business meetings. There you will learn the good and the bad. You will be able to document the struggles and achievements of the congregation. You should not let what you read prejudice you against any persons. Lay leaders can grow in "grace and knowledge" just like pastors.

You can also learn about the past through conversations. Persons will be available to you who have lived the history of the congregation. They carry the history in their memories. If you ask them, they will share it with you. It will not be an objective history like that written by a historian, but it will give you a very personal insight into the past. You may want to have such a conversation with a former pastor or staff member. The longer he served the congregation, the better.

Some of the older members of the congregation will delight in sharing their memories. It will probably vary some from the memory of the former pastor. An afternoon spent with them will leave you a richer person. If they have invested heavily of their lives in the church, they will have a profound appreciation for the ways of God with His church.

Denominational workers have an unusual opportunity to observe a church. They are often involved in both the successes and the failures of the congregation. If you ask them about the past of your new church, you will probably receive a more objective memory of the church.

What Do You Look For?

Unless you know what you are looking for, you may miss it. Let me provide you with a suggested list.

Important People

You will want to know the leaders of the past. I was always humbled by the row of pictures that line the conference room in the First Baptist Church of Lubbock. It is a row of pictures of the pastors who served this congregation in the past. When I saw my picture at the end of the row, I always wondered how it could be. Some of the other congregations I have served had a similar gallery. It is good to have hanging in the gallery of your memory the pictures of the godly laymen and women who worked alongside these pastors. You need to know about the missionaries and preachers who have gone forth from your new church.

Important Events

You want to know about the events that have molded the life of the congregation. You would never fully appreciate the country church in which I grew up, the Chinquapin Grove Baptist Church, Sullivan County, Tennessee, unless you knew about the great revival that swept through the community in the early thirties.

The Beginning of Traditions

Every church has some meaningful traditions. Such traditions help a church develop a sense of identity. God never intended that all churches fit into one neat little pattern. As long as traditions do not impede progress, they can be useful. When I went to Calvary Baptist Church, Lubbock, as pastor, the "tub" offering was such a tradition. We made the most of it as we raised money for the work.

History of Buildings

Each structure has a story to tell. It is usually a story of faith, sacrifice, and dedication. If you are going to shepherd a people, you need to appreciate the symbols of their sacrifice and dedication to God.

The first church I served as pastor, the Biltmore Baptist Church, Elizabethton, Tennessee, is a good example of this. Their first building was constructed out of old material which they personally salvaged out of a building being destroyed to make way for Watagua Lake that would be a part of the TVA system. Men, women, and children cleaned and transported the brick to the new site. It was a symbol of their determination to have a house in which to worship God. Each new pastor needs to know that story.

Expectations

The pastor before you may have left the congregation with a set of expectations. His personal style of ministry set a pattern by which you will be measured. His dreams may have become the dreams of the church. I can still remember the excitement with which the chairman of a pastor search committee shared with me the expectations of his church. He was simply rephrasing a vision that had been left by a popular former pastor. You need to know these things and appreciate them.

How Do You Use What You Learn?

How do you use the fruit of your labor? Let me make a few suggestions. You can add to the list.

As Sermon Material

Illustrations of faith, dedication, and positive churchmanship can be found right before you. You will not only enrich your sermons but also will help the church develop a sense of history.

In Planning For the Future

You should assume that God has been preparing the church for its future. The past is a foundation for the future. One of the positive benefits of this search will uncover some pitfalls you will want to avoid. You will learn of some dreams that have died, as well as some that have become a reality. You will not be able to lead the church where it needs to go until you are familiar with where it has been.

To Influence Present Relationships

If the church knows that you see the hand of God in the past, especially in your predecessors, they will not try to gain your favor by downplaying them. You will not become bigger in the eyes of the church by depreciating what has gone before. You should relate to those of the past with a good awareness of the contribution they have made. You need to make sure that honor is given to those deserving of honor.

No one would question the leadership skills of Moses. You can learn from the effective use he made of history. The first chapters of Deuteronomy are a recitation of history. He re-

An Appreciation

freshed the memory of the congregation of their past so they would be better prepared for their future. Since you have not been on the journey with the new congregation, you must learn their history to be able to lead them today and prepare them for their future.

The backward look is essential for the wise pastoral leader. Even though such a look will require time and effort, the return on your investment will be generous.

4
An Acceptance
A Spiritual Marriage

The relationship between you and the church is similar to the relationship between a husband and wife. The expression "honeymoon" to describe the first months of the pastorate indicates this. The honeymoon time is the awkward period in which both you and the congregation are working hard to please each other. During this period neither party is really relaxed or comfortable. When the honeymoon is over, the real pastor and the real church begin to emerge. The big question is, Will the pastor and people still like each other when the honeymoon is over?

In a good marriage the honeymoon is followed by something more exciting—a period of mutual acceptance. This happens when the newlyweds discover that they can relax and be themselves. They can be less than perfect and still be loved. If this mutual acceptance never develops, the marriage is in trouble. The same thing can happen in a good pastorate. The day comes when the pastor knows that he does not have to be the perfect pastor to be loved and the church knows that the pastor is committed to them even though they do have faults. When you sense that you are moving toward such a mutual acceptance, you know that you are on the way to a glad beginning.

The Necessity

The necessity for this acceptance is rooted in the nature of the relationship. The relationship between you and the church is one of trust, just like the relationship between a husband and wife. You will never be effective as the pastor until this trust relationship develops. It will do no good for you to demand it of the people. It is something that most congregations will give freely when you have demonstrated that you are trustworthy.

Human nature makes this process a necessity. You are not a perfect pastor and never will be. Evidently some former pastors came closer than you! The search committee often forgets to tell the congregation that you are not perfect. They want to make themselves look good so they tend to oversell the new pastor. They conveniently forget to tell about some of the weaknesses their research uncovered. They want the congregation to believe that they have found "the man of God" for their church. What they forget is that you do not have to be perfect to be "the man of God."

The church you have accepted is not a perfect church, and never will be. The search committee may forget to tell the prospective pastor about the problems of the church. They do not mention the negative thinkers, power brokers, neurotics, and generally unpleasant people in the church. To listen to the committee, you would think everyone was ready to see the church grow, to take the Great Commission seriously, and to follow their pastor to the end of the world.

This makes the first months of your pastorate interesting. They will be months of discovery! The church will discover that you are very human. While you are a man of God, you are still a man. Not all of your sermons should be nominated for "Sermon of the Year." You probably have at least one irritating mannerism. Your children tend to be pretty normal—

much like the deacons' children. You also begin to discover the truth about the church. It is not unlike the church you just left. Not everybody votes yes just because the pastor suggests a project or plan. Some deacons talk too much, and some talk too little. Some people have an opinion on everything and are quick to share it. You learn that you must have the approval of certain persons if a new program is to have a chance. Not everyone is excited about missions and evangelism, especially if they are expected to do it or help pay for it. In other words the church is just a normal New Testament church—a congregation of sinners depending totally on God's mercy and grace. Since you are a redeemed sinner pastoring a congregation of redeemed sinners, it will take a while for this acceptance to take place. We have difficulty accepting the fact that we are all sinners before God.

Only when you know the truth about each other, can you and the church accept each other. It is a relationship that manifests the grace of God at work in our midst.

The Product of Time

You must be willing to wait for this acceptance. It requires more than a unanimous call from the church. Even your full commitment to their invitation to be their pastor will not make it happen. These two events just put you into a position where it can happen. Most studies indicate that two or three years are required for this relationship to fully mature. The length of this acceptance process will vary from church to church.

The church may be a divided church. The internal division may be rather obvious, or it may be camouflaged. The first three churches I served had just terminated the pastor before me. I did not have to ask if there was division in the church, I could feel it every time the church met. Before I could be genuinely accepted as their pastor, a measure of internal healing had to take place. This required time.

The church may be a grieving church. When a church has enjoyed a good relationship with a pastor, and he leaves, they grieve like a widow. They feel pretty sure that no man will ever be able to take the place of their beloved pastor who just left. This grief may also include some anger toward him for "deserting" them. Until they have passed through this grief process, they are not ready to receive you as their new pastor. This can be a tough time for you as the new pastor. Sensing that a church is still preoccupied with the former pastor can be very distressing. If a real acceptance is to take place, you must be patient. All of this requires time.

The church may be a demoralized church. If your predecessor left under unusual circumstances, the church may be down on itself. Unfortunately, a pastor sometimes falls into public sin and brings reproach upon himself and the church he serves. The church feels betrayed. They are much like the woman who has caught her husband being unfaithful. She may be able to trust a man again, but it will take time. The demoralized church is not capable of giving the trust that makes acceptance possible, yet.

Without any unusual circumstances, acceptance will take an extended period of time to occur. This period must be one of prayerful waiting, faithful service, and hopeful expectation.

The Product of Trust

Trust is developed through shared experiences. As you begin to enter into the joys, sorrows, and struggles of the people, trust will begin to develop. As you weep with them in their crises and rejoice with them at their weddings, they will begin to feel "this man really does love us." After a while, as a by-product of good pastoral ministry, trust develops. This trust makes acceptance possible.

Trust may be encouraged by a shared crisis. You do not pray for these, but they do happen sometimes. One pastor went to a church that had gone through the trauma of having their pastor forsake his wife for a secretary. The new pastor found the church short on trust. However, when a terrible fire burned their beautiful sanctuary to the ground and the pastor led them through the crisis with faith and love, trust was born. This trust resulted in a beautiful acceptance between pastor and people which made a long and fruitful ministry possible.

I experienced this in a milder form. The church had considered building a new auditorium under the former pastor. For a number of reasons this dream was never realized. When I became pastor the question of whether to build was very much alive in the congregation. We appointed a committee to make a thorough study and to bring back a recommendation to the church. Their study resulted in a recommendation that the old sanctuary be renovated. They demonstrated how this would meet the needs of the congregation, and would result in considerable savings to the congregation. The night the church enthusiastically approved the recommendation of the committee, they accepted me as their pastor. Even though I was different from the pastor they had loved for many years, they now trusted me as their pastor. From that day onward the relationship was different. It had never been bad, it had been like an awkward honeymoon, but now it was good. This became the basis of some very happy years of ministry.

This process will bring you and the church to a new understanding. The people will understand that you do not have to be perfect to be God's man for their church. They learn that God has always done His work through very imperfect human beings. You begin to understand that the church does not have to be perfect to be the people of God. Even though Jesus called the seven churches of Asia Minor "golden lampstands," each of them was flawed in some serious way. Their flaws did not detract from their value to the risen Lord who stood in their midst.

The Fruit

This acceptance will make venturing together possible. You can begin to lead the congregation to make some needed changes. Some pastors have mistakenly believed that the only time to accomplish change is during the honeymoon period. They fear that when the newness wears off the relationship the church will be unwilling to make changes. The opposite is true. Changes made during the early days may be a hindrance to acceptance every happening. Once you have been accepted by the congregation, you can lead them to do almost anything that is for their good. There is even good evidence that you may be able to lead them to do things that are not for their good.

I have seen this relationship develop to the point that my influence over the congregation was frightening. They trusted me so much that they did not think to challenge some of my half-baked propositions. This will surely make you more cautious in making proposals to the church.

You will also be able to lead them to venture forth in greater ministry. This is why the longer pastorate is usually the more fruitful pastorate. Many pastors leave before they ever get to the point of effective leadership with the congregation. In the atmosphere of mutual acceptance, both the pastor and the people will be at their best in creativity. The congregation will be free to express themselves and to use the gifts of God. The pastor will not be afraid to propose something that is bold and daring!

Freedom may be the best word to describe what happens when this acceptance takes place. You and the people are then free to devote your full energies to the task. You do not have to spend all of your energy working on your relationship. This is something to be coveted for every church and pastor.

What can you do to encourage such a relationship?
1. Believe that it is possible.
2. Ask God for it expectantly.
3. Be aware of the forces that are preventing it.
4. Be patient! Be patient!
5. Be candid with the church about your desire for it.
6. Be faithful in the work of the ministry.

As I reflect on the pastorates I have enjoyed, a special sense of gratitude wells up in my heart. A special relationship developed with each of them. Though a different pattern developed in each case, a time came when we experienced mutual acceptance.

While this acceptance is a gracious work of God, you can do things that will enhance His work. Begin the new pastorate with a commitment to do your part. God must do the rest!

5
An Understanding
An Agreement About Ministry

Whose ministry will you perform in the new church? Will you fulfill the ministry to which you feel you have been called, or will you be controlled by the expectations of the congregation? What you desire is an *intentional ministry*. You will want to be free to give expression to your own sense of calling and the spiritual gifts God has given to you. If this is to happen, you and the congregation must come to an agreement about ministry. It will probably never be a formal agreement, but there must be such an agreement.

The way to achieve such an agreement is called *negotiation*. You may not be comfortable with the word, but it is what you do. Negotiation is made necessary by the differences in understanding between you and the congregation. A number of influences have helped you form your own understanding of your ministry and your own set of priorities. You have been influenced by your training and your personal Bible study. You have been influenced by your church experiences. You have been influenced by the models that you have adopted. Because of these influences and others, you bring to the new pastorate a rather clear picture of the ministry you desire.

But the church has a different idea. They have a set of expectations for their new pastor. They have been exposed to different church experiences. Each pastor of the past has made his contribution to their set of expectations. They, too, have their model, and it is different in many cases. Many times their expectations have been influenced by their vocational experiences. While they do not understand the task of the pastor fully, they interpret it in light of their own work. I can still remember the deacon who always called me "Coach." Since coaching was his work, he interpreted my work in light of his vocation. I was the "head coach" to him. To some degree the church will have been influenced by the Bible. They will expect you to have the boldness of Elijah, the wisdom of Solomon, the tenderness of Jeremiah, the energy of Paul, and the leadership abilities of Simon Peter. Most studies have revealed that no mortal man could ever measure up to the expectations of the average congregation.

What do you do then? You must reach an agreement with the congregation about the nature of your ministry among them. You cannot throw away your own sense of ministry and try to measure up to all of their expectations. This would result in ministerial suicide! But neither can you ignore their expectations! You must negotiate!

Reached Unconsciously

As I look back over my first pastorates, I am aware that we reached an agreement without using the word *negotiation*. We worked out the basic elements of an intentional ministry without every knowing this was something we were supposed to do. This is true for most pastors. It is an unconscious process.

My first pastorate was with a congregation that had been served by some good men. One of my predecessors had been a man who was committed to pastoral visitation. He had literally gone from house to house. Both the members and the prospects were visited regularly. My models for ministry had not been strong in this area of ministry. Most of their visitation had been done in response to a crisis or a request. They had given more emphasis to the preaching ministry of the pastor.

One day one of the older deacons of the church took me aside to share with me a concern. Some of the congregation expected more visitation from their young pastor than I was doing. After some good counsel from him, I began to devote more time to pastoral visitation. Growing out of this experience, pastoral visitation has taken a prominent place in my intentional ministry. Even though we were not aware of it, a process of negotiation was taking place. We came to an agreement about ministry, and I was a better pastor as a result.

So, whether or not you commit yourself to a formal process of negotiation, if you are to have a glad beginning, some will take place. If it is consciously and deliberately done, it will bear better fruit.

Begins with the Search Committee

You understand about negotiations with the search committee. You know how to come to an understanding about how much vacation you have, what the salary will be, where you will live, and matters like this. While these things are important, the more important thing is the type of ministry you will have in the church.

You should be prepared for your meeting with the committee. You should be prepared to ask them questions that will put you in touch with their expectations. You have opportunity to learn something about them from a former pastor, denominational leaders, or another knowledgeable person before the meeting. This will help you formulate the questions that you will want to ask. You should also be prepared to share with them your own understanding of your ministry. You should be ready to give an answer to any question concerning the ministry God has given to you. You should make clear your priorities, your practices, and anything else that will help them know your expectations.

Your discussions with the search committee would be greatly enhanced by a role description. The committee will probably not have one. In more than thirty years of ministry, and after scores of contacts with such committees, I have yet to talk with a committee that had any kind of a written statement that expressed their expectations. They assume that you know what they will expect the pastor to do. This is not a safe assumption. You can help the discussion by preparing a written statement of your understanding of your role as a pastor, making copies available to the committee, and discussing the statement.

The role description would not be a detailed job description, but would rather be a statement of what you perceive the role of the pastor to be. It would probably include a statement about your role as preacher, administrator, counselor, program leader, and evangelist. It would probably include a statement about how you would expect to function in these different roles. It would surely include a statement about your understanding of pastoral authority since this has become such a divisive issue in some churches.

You should make clear to the committee which aspects of the statement are negotiable. This will give you a basis for a healthy discussion with the committee and will initiate that negotiations that must be a part of a glad beginning.

Most pastors could write an interesting book about their experiences with search committees. You can usually identify the problems in the church by the questions that are asked. You can also usually make a pretty good profile of the last pastor from the questions. One committee was more concerned about my attitude toward the church having a softball team than they were my view of the Holy Scriptures.

The last pastor had disapproved of the church having a softball team. To his surprise, softball had been important to the church! They were not willing to negotiate this issue. Another committee was more concerned about my health than anything else. Their last pastor had been sickly. While some committees are refreshingly prepared for their work, you have to be prepared to lead the discussion toward an understanding.

When your discussions with them have been completed, the committee should have a fairly clear understanding of you and your ministry. They should know your doctrinal positions, your attitudes toward the denomination and its programs, your patterns of work, your priorities, the role your family plays in your ministry, and anything else that will help them understand what you would intend to do if you became their pastor. You should have a good understanding of their expectations of their pastor and what his role will be in their church. If their ideas and yours are not compatible, you must either negotiate with them or terminate the discussion.

A word of warning. Some pastors have been so anxious to impress a committee that they have told the committee only what they thought the committee wanted to hear. This can lead to serious problems later. If your being open with the committee concerning your style of ministry and expectations will close the door, it probably needs to be closed.

Include the Leadership

In most cases you will want an opportunity to visit with the leaders of the church before you accept the invitation to become pastor. This can be the time when you begin to come to an agreement about ministry. While it may be overshadowed by the need to get acquainted, it needs to be on the agenda. This can include a private time of discussion with the staff. It should definitely include a time of discussion with the deacons and Church Council. Though the discussion cannot be as in-depth as with the search committee, it can follow the same pattern. You should use it as an opportunity to introduce them to your priorities and goals as a pastor and should allow them to ask you any question that they might have.

The early days of your pastorate will be a continuance of this pursuit of an understanding. As you meet with different committees and groups in the church, you will be introducing them to your goals and priorities as a pastor. It may not be on the official agenda, but it will be a concern to the different groups. This is the time for you to help them to adopt your view of the ministry and negotiate any points where you encounter resistance. They must know that you are a person with deep convictions about what you are suppose to do as a pastor but that you are always open to any idea that will help you do it better. Convictions with a teachable spirit is an unbeatable combination.

Another word of warning! You should not assume that all of the changing has to be on the part of the congregation. The church can contribute something to your understanding of ministry that will enrich it. Each church I have served has helped me to grow in some aspect of my ministry. My growth usually has been at some point of expectation that they had of what a pastor should be. Rather than negotiate about their expectation, I have adopted it. In doing this, I became a better pastor. Indeed, this whole process of negotiation will be a time of growth for both you and the church.

May Be Preceded by Tension

Some tensions should be ignored. Sometimes your approach to ministry will lead to unrest simply because it is new. If given enough time, the approach to ministry will vindicate itself. A confrontation over the unrest may put the unsettled in a position of having to defend their ideas. This can lead to a settled opposition to you and your ministry. It is just better to leave some things in the hand of the Lord.

But some points of tension will need to be confronted. When you become aware that your style of ministry has led to a serious disappointment to someone, the best approach may be confrontation. By confrontation I mean a heart-to-heart talk with the person where you will seek an understanding of why he feels the way he does. You will attempt to interpret your own approach to ministry to the person. Several such "friendly chats" may be necessary in the early days of a pastorate. The person involved may never realize what you are doing, but you know. You are attempting to negotiate an approach to ministry; you are attempting to establish an intentional ministry.

These tensions can be healthy. They are at least a reflection of someone taking ministry of the church seriously. Any pastor would rather deal with such tensions than with apathy or indifference. When such tensions are handled creatively, both you and the church will profit.

The business world knows more about this process of negotiation than we do in the church. You may want to equip yourself in this skill. How open you are about what you are doing will depend on your own temperament and how confident you feel about your negotiation skills. But you must do it! Without an agreement with the church and its leaders about the kind of ministry you will have, you will never experience a glad beginning.

Many a pastor has made the mistake of assuming everyone understood the type of ministry he desired. The pastor is then frustrated when he begins to encounter resistance to his programs and ministry. You will not be able to eliminate all of the resistance, but an intelligent attempt at negotiation will prevent much of it. This would seem to fit comfortably into the biblical calls for honesty, openness, and understanding. It is much better to prayerfully negotiate than to manipulate or frustrate.

6
A Vision
Establishing Some Goals

Goals are important in the ministry of your church. The churches that make the greatest impact for the kingdom of God are marked by the goals to which they have committed themselves.

While the ultimate objectives of the church never may be achieved, you need some goals that can be achieved. Our ultimate objectives are to glorify God, to preach the gospel to every person in every nation, and to present each person to Christ at His coming fully matured. These are always challenges for which we strive. Long- and short-term goals can break these challenges into segments that we can achieve.

Goals will help you and your church achieve unity. They will give you a basis for planning and will encourage efficiency. Goals will help you establish proper priorities and give you a standard by which to measure progress. They will motivate you to exert a greater effort.

So, as you begin your new pastorate, goals must be a concern. You and the congregation will need some goals to which you can commit yourselves.

Inherited Goals

Part of the heritage you receive from the former pastor are goals. The measure of vision present will be a reflection of the ministry of former pastors. This can sometimes be a problem. If the former pastor was a strong personality, he may have imposed his vision on the church. I remember visiting with one search committee where this had happened. The pastor who had just left had been judged by his inability to achieve the goals he had inherited from the former pastor. That pastor had been a strong preacher and leader. He had dreamed of an auditorium that would seat thousands. The search committee was still looking for someone to make that dream a reality even though they really did not need such a worship center.

However, you should not reject a goal simply because it grew out of the ministry of the former pastor. You may adopt some of the goals established by former pastors. It is not bad just because the former pastor thought of it. God does not work out a new plan for a church just because it changes pastors. Rather, God's plan for each church is an unfolding plan; the pastor is only one part of it. Most things are still the same after the change of pastors. The great objectives of the church have not changed. The basic community in which the church ministers has not changed. The tools available to the church will not have changed dramatically. The difference will probably be how you attempt to achieve the goals rather than the goals themselves. Your gifts and experiences will be different, so you will probably want to go about it in a different way.

You will be able to identify some goals as you go through a long-range planning process. You should make every attempt to get rid of the inadequate goals without questioning the leadership of the former pastor or the decision of a prior planning committee of the church. This is something that would probably best be handled through a long-range planning committee.

Long-Range Planning

By long-range planning, I mean a process that would involve a significant number of lay leaders with you for an in-depth study of the history of your church, a careful look at your present situation, and a projection of goals and plans for the next three to five years. Unless the church has just completed such a process before you arrive, this could be a good place to begin. I have done so with good benefits in the last two churches I have served.

If the church has just gone through such a process, you should acquaint yourself with the plan before you become pastor. You should feel comfortable with the general direction of it. With the help of a standing long-range planning committee, you can lead the church to amend or enlarge its plan. You would not need to start from the beginning in the process.

Not every plan labeled "long-range plan" qualifies as such. Some are limited to projected building plans. Projected building plans have no significance apart from the projected development and growth of the church. You will want to make sure that the church actually has what it thinks it has. If the plan does not set goals and have specific plans by which the goals are going to be achieved, you do not have a *plan*.

What will a true long-range plan give you and your church? It will give you a clearly written, objective statement for your church. To have the church make a meaningful adoption of such a statement can be helpful. Many members have never seriously thought about the ultimate objective of their church.

The plan will give you an extensive list of the needs that the committee has discovered in your community and church. This, too, can be an eye-opener for the congregation.

The plan will give you a few goals that relate to the objective of the church. These goals will be achievable, measurable, and challenging. To be achievable, there cannot be too many of them.

The plan will give you a set of specific plans and strategies by which the goals will be achieved. These will be assigned to a specific person or group for the action. They will also have a date by which the work should be finished.

Will such a plan be helpful to you as the new pastor? I believe that it will. Consider these things:
1. A long-range plan will involve you with a significant number of church leaders in the formation of a vision statement.
2. It will help you and the church evaluate the effectiveness of all the present programs of the church.
3. It will force you and the church to plan together.
4. It will help you and the church establish some priorities together.
5. It will enable the church to address some of its continuing problems.
6. It will clarify and simplify the work of the church.

How would you begin such a long-range plan? You should first acquaint yourself with the whole process. For example, you could purchase a long-range planning guide that has been prepared by the Church Administration Department of The Sunday School Board of the Southern Baptist Convention. It will outline for you the whole process step-by-step. Then you should lead the church to elect a long-range planning committee, which includes some of your most mature church leaders. You may want to secure the help of an outside consultant. Someone on the staff of your denomination should be able to suggest someone to you. The consultant would be able to keep pressure on you to follow the plan and to avoid some of the deadly shortcuts. Then you should be prepared to invest some major blocks of time for several months to complete such a plan. It will involve some hard work, but it will be worth it.

Lead the Way to a Vision

Whether or not the church does a long-range plan, the pastor is still the key. If the church ever has a vision, it will begin with him.

This follows the biblical pattern. The great faith chapter of Hebrews 11 acknowledges to events of congregational faith. The writer indicated that the congregation passed through the Red Sea by faith (v. 29). He then reminded readers that the Hebrews also overthrew the city of Jericho by faith (v. 30). In both cases, the congregation achieved the impossible by faith. In both cases, a bold leader challenged the people to attempt the impossible. It is doubtful that they would have ever ventured forth to walk through the sea without Moses. Joshua was definitely the faith leader at Jericho. Studies of growing, effective churches in our day have revealed the importance of the role of the pastor-leader. There is almost always a pastor with a vision before there is a congregation with a vision.

You can help form a vision in the church through your preaching. One pastor went to an old church that had lost its vision. He spent his first months as pastor preaching through the Acts of the Apostles expositorily. He helped the church gain a new understanding of its resources in the Holy Spirit and the gospel. He helped them gain a new appreciation for the evangelistic task of the church. He helped them experience a new level of expectation for the church. The church experienced a new excitement about being the people of God. All of this led to a period of record-breaking growth for the church. The pulpit is still a good place for the pastor to help form the vision that is needed.

If a long-range planning committee is elected, you will be able to have effective input. You may have to lead the committee in some periods of Bible study that confront them with God's vision for His church. You can make sure that they become familiar with some of the exciting things other churches are doing. You will allow the committee to benefit from your years of experience and study. While they will do the work and make the report, you will be influencing their work each step of the way.

If you see the committee making some mistakes, you can usually prevent it by asking the right questions. You will be able to correct their course without opposing their work, in most cases. Usually providing added information or helping them gain another perspective will be enough. In the early days of your pastorate, they will be anxious to listen to your counsel. You can do this without corrupting it into the pastor's long-range plan for the church.

The sooner you help the congregation begin to catch a new vision, the better it will be for a glad beginning. Initial enthusiasm will soon disappear if goals have not been established and plans for the work have not been made. While this part of the work will never be finished, it can add significantly to the beginning of your work with the church.

7
A Plan
Staying with the Basics

Dr. Wilbur Turner gave me some of the best advice I ever received. He was the director of missions for the Lubbock Baptist Association in Texas at the time. I was a young pastor serving my first church after seminary in his association. The Lord had been pleased to prosper my work with the church. A significant healing had taken place in the fellowship of the church. A new excitement had come into the life of the church and we were experiencing good growth. The Lord used this to attract the attention of a pastor search committee from a larger church.

When the search committee from the larger church approached me, I was both excited and frightened. The size of the congregation bothered me. I had grown up in a country church and had pastored three smaller congregations, so pastoring in a city worried me. This church had staff members, secretaries, a full-time custodian, committees, and a lot of things about which I knew nothing. When I went to Dr. Turner for some counsel, what he said encouraged me greatly. He simply said, "D. L., when you make the move, just stick to the basics. The things that made you a good pastor in the smaller church will work in the larger church." He was right! There are some basics that you do not change when you change churches.

The time of transition can be a time of evaluation, but it

will not be a time to change the basics. You may want to correct the way you have been doing some of them, but some things do not change.

Preaching

You will still be the preacher in the new church. It will still demand a priority in your life and ministry. Your basic approach to preaching probably will not change when you change churches. While you will always be looking for ways to improve your preaching, your basic commitment to communicate the Word of God through preaching will not change.

One pitfall to avoid in a new pastorate relates to preaching. You will be tempted to coast for a while by preaching some old sermons. Almost none of my sermons deserve to be preached again without improvement! Are you sure about yours? One of the worst indictments I have ever heard against a pastor came from a very sensitive layman. He said of his pastor as he closed a pastorate of more than five years, "I don't believe he preached a fresh sermon all the time he was here." The layman may have been right. If so, it was tragic. You know that God did something fresh in the pastor's life from time to time. My own experience is that not to do fresh preparation takes some of the excitement out of preaching. I need that time of disciplined preparation week by week.

Your preaching in the new church should soon begin to reflect the needs of your new congregation. While there will be many things that will be the same, this congregation will have its own set of needs. They will begin to respond to you when they know that you are faithfully and lovingly seeking to apply the eternal Word of God to their lives.

One other pitfall to avoid. Do not overload your people with illustrations based on the lives of the people you have just left! This is always a temptation. You need to remember that someone will have a relative or friend in the congregation you just left—they might just begin to compare notes on some of your stories. This might prove to be an embarrassment.

The new congregation will get its first impression from your preaching. This makes it important that you come to them with a fresh word for the Lord service after service in the first months of your ministry. In time they will know you as pastor in other aspects of your ministry, but at first your preaching sets the tone. You do not have to be a superstar in preaching, but you do need to be carefully prepared for each opportunity. This is truly a basic.

Study Habits

A disciplined pattern of study is basic for a glad beginning. The early days of the new pastorate is the time to put in place your regular times for study. You should inform the congregation about these times of study. If the church has a weekly newsletter, you can do it through the pastor's column. If you do not have such a mailout, you can do it from the pulpit. They should learn from you just how important you feel this time of study is to you.

My pattern for work has been to devote the mornings to study. During my ten-year pastorate in Fort Worth, I had my study at home. In the other places, I have studied at the church. The dynamics of the local situation will help you determine which is the best for you. The morning study time has been profitable for me.

A friend of mine who has been a good pastoral leader devotes one day out of the week to sermon preparation. He usually takes Tuesday. On that day he will be away from the church for the entire day. He has a cabin in which he keeps his basic library for study. The whole day is devoted to study and prayer in preparation for his preaching responsibilities. It will be supplemented by other times during the week.

If your new church has never recognized that study is a basic part of the pastor's work, you will need to explain the need and responsibility of study. You may want to remind them of the pattern of the early church leaders who felt the need for such protected time (Acts 6:4).

The excitement of the new pastorate can easily crowd out study time. You will have many people to see and many things to do that may seem more important. You will be better served by sticking to the basics.

Pastoral Visitation

Wise pastors still do pastoral visitation. It has become more difficult in the urban setting where many of us work, but it is not impossible. Kenneth Callahan, a Methodist church leader set a high goal for pastoral visitation. He suggested that the pastor spend one hour in pastoral visitation for each minute he preaches on Sunday morning. If this were required, it might result in shorter sermons! Callahan would include both the visits made to the church family and those made to the unchurched. This may be too much for most of us, but we surely need to set a challenging goal for ourselves.

Consistent pastoral visitation will require planning. You will need to block out specific times for visitation on your schedule. This should be done in the light of your own community—visit when you are most likely to find people at home. In my case, this has meant devoting at least one evening per week to prospect visitation and a major part of Saturday to the same. You can do some afternoon visitation with the elderly or shut-ins or crisis needs in the church family.

Pastoral visitation bears good fruit. It helps build a good pastoral relationship with the people. It assures the congregation of your concern for their welfare. It keeps you in touch with the needs of your people—this will make you a better preacher on Sunday. You will be following the example of the Chief Shepherd who spent much of His time among the sheep.

Crisis Ministry

You must be available to your people in the time of crisis. This includes times of illness, death, unemployment, marital difficulties, and many others. You must be available to offer counsel, prayer, support, and encouragement. Through your ministry in the time of crisis, you earn the right to be the leader of the sheep. Trust is developed as you walk with people in the valley.

A word of caution: As the new pastor, you should seek counsel from someone who has ministered in the community before you. He will be able to inform you of any unique expectations that may be associated with the pastoral ministry there. Funeral practices vary from community to community. You can save yourself some embarrassment and missed opportunities for ministry by becoming informed.

Every pastor knows that crises do not always come at the right time. How you handle them can be important! Recently I encountered a bitter man who had been neglected, at least in his eyes, because the pastor was involved in other things when death came to his family. The sheep need the shepherd in the valley! You cannot be God to them, but you do represent His presence to them in a very personal way.

The sheep will forgive many shortcomings if you are faithful to them in their time of crisis. This is a basic!

Program Leadership

While you are called to be the pastor-teacher of the congregation, you must also give attention to program leadership. In most cases, the success of any program is directly related to the amount of leadership the pastor gives to it. This does not mean that you do all of the work, but it does mean that you must be perceived as the leader. If you are viewed as not valuing the program, it will be dead in the water! So you need to evaluate carefully the programs of the church and be aware of your relationship to them. You must decide which of these programs are essential for the health and progress of the church. If they are essential, you must give yourself to leading them. There may be some that you should allow to die a natural death.

Surely you will put your Sunday School on the essential list. In those churches where the Sunday School is a basic strategy for church growth and ministry, it is surely essential. As the Sunday School goes so will everything else in the church. It will be important for you to be publicly and privately committed to the Sunday School.

This commitment should involve you in the recruitment of workers, in the enlargement of the organization, in the training of workers, in the provision of space for expansion, and in the leadership of the outreach visitation. None of this will happen as it should without you!

Any pastor can be prepared for this role of leadership. By attending Sunday School conferences for pastors in your association, by attending a Sunday School week at a national conference center, or by just reading some of the basic books on Sunday School work, you can prepare yourself. It would also be helpful to spend some time with a pastor who has been successful in this aspect of his ministry. You can learn from him.

You will make a mistake if you see such program leadership as being beneath your calling. It is a part of the oversight responsibilities of the local church pastor.

Equipping Activities

You are to equip the saints for the work of the ministry (Eph. 4:12). This is the primary reason the ascended Lord placed you in the body. How do you perform this equipping assignment? You can do a major part of it through your regular preaching and teaching ministry, but some of it has to become practical work. You need to identify the areas in which your people need to be equipped and then commit yourself to do it through your preaching-teaching ministry and through designed practical activities.

One practical activity may be establishing a Continuous Witness Training (CWT) program to equip laypeople to do personal evangelism. It can be as practical as scheduling a Spiritual Awakening Seminar to motivate and equip the people for prayer. It may be as practical as leading or enlisting a leader for a teacher improvement seminar. It may be that you will want to establish a leadership training program.

These are basics! If you are to lead the church, you must be sure that it is equipped to go where God wants it to go. Do not make them feel guilty for not doing things you have not equipped them to do!

Prayer

Prayer is a basic. It is basic for your personal and ministerial life. The excitement and pressures of a new pastorate can devastate your own devotional life. If it does, it will cut you off from your source of strength. So you need to double up on your personal devotional life during the early days of a pastorate.

The new pastorate will also require some changes in your pastoral prayer life. You will want to establish a pattern of praying regularly for a new set of leaders. I have found it helpful to pray for my deacons and key leaders by name each week. I have also found it helpful to visit the empty classrooms of our Sunday School and pray by name for the people who teach and work there. Then, you will want some system by which you will pray for the individuals who make up your congregation. This will make you a better person, even as they are blessed through your prayers.

The new pastorate will also require the beginning of a new prayer list for the unsaved. This can be exciting. As you meet new people and begin to witness in the new field of service, you will find many unsaved people. Few of them will ever be won without someone praying for them. You can lift some of them up to the Lord regularly.

It should become obvious to your new church soon that you are a person of prayer. A praying pastor will soon produce a praying church—and such a church will soon begin to change the world. Prayer has to be a basic.

As you begin this new assignment, stick with the basics! You will want to try something new, but do not do it at the expense of the basics. Some football games are won on trick plays, but most of them are won by the basics. The same is true in pastoral ministry.

Part II
A Gracious Ending

8
Leadership
Signs You Should Move

To move or not to move? This question has caused pastors many sleepless nights. It may even make a person wish he were in a denomination where someone else makes this decision. He wants to be in the will of God for his life, but how can he be sure? What if he makes a mistake?

While there are no unmistakable signs about when it is time to move, there are some signs that have been helpful to many pastors. When faced with the question of whether a move is in order, it is time to do some prayerful reflection.

Misleading Signs

Many pastors have made serious mistakes because they moved for the wrong reason. You need to make sure that your reason for moving is a spiritually and vocationally valid one.

Problems in the church are not a sign that you should move. This would include "problem" people who are making the work difficult. Any pastor who perseveres in a church will go through some trying times. These trying times may be totally unrelated to his effectiveness as a spiritual leader. It is some encouragement to know that even the apostle Paul knew the pain of facing discouragement in the church. Not everyone in the churches he served was excited about his leadership. Indeed, the problems may be a sign the pastor should stay. Some churches have been destroyed by problems because no pastor would stay long enough to deal with them. When they appeared, the pastor would move on. The problems may be nothing more than growing pains. To have a long and fruitful pastorate means that pastor and congregation must continue to grow.

The problems may be caused by "problem" people. Usually such persons need loving confrontation—not fearful avoidance. If you are moving to avoid such persons, they probably have a twin in the church to which you are moving. Each congregation has its share of such "disturbers of the fellowship." Their presence could be a divinely arranged opportunity for you to grow in grace and patience. God surely wants us to learn something through such people. If they do nothing else, they will surely have a positive impact on our prayer lives.

Every pastor can be grateful that a search committee did not come at certain points in his ministry. He would have moved without much reflection. He would also have missed some of the best days in his ministry which came after he had gone through the difficult times. So problems are not a sure sign that you should move.

Spiritual dryness is not a good sign that you should move. By spiritual dryness, I mean a time when you have lost some of your enthusiasm for what you are doing, which is usually accompanied by a slowdown in the life of the church. You have not quit praying and working, but you just do not seem to be making much progress personally or in your work. In such a time it is easy to think that a change of scenery might help.

However, a study of pastoral relations in a longer pastorate reveals that there are discernable cycles through which pastorates go. Many of the seemingly dry seasons generally are followed by times of great fruitfulness and blessings for both the church and the pastor. You must at least consider the possibility that your work is just going through such a cycle.

If you keep a spiritual diary, you may become aware of the cycles in your own life. Every day is not meant to be spent on the mountaintop. Not every Sunday needs to be a repeat of Pentecost. Reading the biographies and autobiographies of the great pastors of the past can be helpful. You cannot read about a Spurgeon, Maclaren, or Truett without being encouraged. They went through times of "dryness" in their work. You might even be going through one of the life cycles which is affecting how you feel about what you are doing.

Some reading on the life cycles we go through might give you some insight into your journey. James W. Fowler's *Stages of Faith* has helpfully related the cycles to spiritual development. If your unrest is a part of such a life cycle, you will need more than new scenery to find fulfillment.

In such a season of life, you need to address the cause of the dryness rather than look for another pastorate. You may need a vacation or a retreat more than you need a new church. A continuing education experience at a seminary might do wonders for you. When Elijah thought he was ready for a new pastorate, the Lord sent him on an extended period of rest and relaxation in a cave. After a period of rest, the Lord sent him back to work with the same unlikely congregation. While the negative feelings you have about your life and work can be a matter for serious concern, you probably need more than a new address.

An "open door" is not a sign you should move. By an "open door" I mean a search committee of at least five people from a larger church that pays a higher salary that is extending you an invitation to become their pastor. While such an experience will always get your attention, it does not mean that you have received a heavenly mandate to move.

The apostle Paul learned that more than an open door is

necessary to constitute a call. When he came to Mysia, Bithynia looked like an open door. It appeared to be the best place to take the gospel next. "But the Spirit of Jesus would not allow them" (Acts 16:7, NIV). Exactly how the Spirit did this restraining is not given. It may have been nothing more than an inner restraint from the Lord. It could have been some unexpected circumstance that blocked the way. What we know is that the Lord wanted Paul to go to Philippi. So what appears to be an open door, may not really be the right door.

I experienced something like this in the early days of my ministry. I resigned a good congregation when I finished college so I could move to Texas and pursue theological education. After a few months, I found being a churchless pastor a difficult experience. I wanted to be a pastor more than anything else in the world. One weekend I preached for a small rural church not far from the seminary. They indicated that they wanted to call me to be their pastor. It sure looked like an open door to me. Everything in me wanted to respond, "Yes, I will do it." However, as I prayed about it, I felt a real restraint on my inner spirit. I knew in my heart that this was not the place for me. After I declined the open door, I really went into a period of depression. I did not understand why the Lord would let me be confronted with an open door and then restrain me.

A few weeks later I understood! A church that provided a much larger challenge called me to be its pastor. It was large enough to provide us a home and a salary to meet our basic needs while I went to school. And did we ever need it! I did not know it, but we were about to lose our only source of income due to an unexpected pregnancy. My wife had been teaching school and, according to school policy, pregnant women could not teach. You need more than an open door to constitute a reason for moving.

An obvious need is not a sign you should move. You may find yourself confronted with a church that has great need and opportunity. If you move every time you are confronted with such need, you will get to know the men at the moving company better than you do your deacons. When you move, it should be for the right reasons.

Signs to Consider

If you have lost your place of leadership in the church, it may be time to move. There are a number of things that can erode the leadership position of the pastor. You may have made some mistakes that have shaken the confidence of the people in your leadership ability. Most of us have reason to thank God for the forgiveness extended to us by the people we have served, but sometimes you may not receive such forgiveness from them. You may have lost the support of a portion of the church because of some decision that you led the church to make. The action may have been the right thing for the church, but the wrong thing for your personal ministry with the church. Regardless of the cause, if you do not have the trust of the church, your days of effectiveness are over.

Unfortunately you may be the last to realize that you have lost your leadership position. Lay people are not always able to confront their pastor with their doubts about his leadership. They do not want to lay their hands on "God's anointed," so they pull back in their support. Every pastor needs a small group of trusted persons in the congregation who will be honest with him. You need their input about how your ministry is being received. You need them to make you aware of blind spots that you may have developed. You should not be the last person to learn that a serious breach has developed or that a sizable portion of your leaders think that it is time for you to move.

The loss of your place of leadership will require some serious and honest reflection. If you come to a firm conviction that you are no longer an effective leader, it could be a sign that you should prayerfully consider another pastorate. However, do not make the move until you have honestly determined why you lost this place of leadership. What could you have done differently? Was it because of a faulty leadership style? Was it because of a fault in the fellowship of the church? Learn all you can from such a painful experience—you surely do not want to repeat it.

A fulfilled vision can be a sign that it is time to move. God brings different persons to a church to accomplish different things. There can come a time in your life in which you feel that you have accomplished your mission with a particular congregation. This does not mean that the work is done—just that your portion of the work is done.

I have experienced this. After pastoring a church for almost ten years, I found myself at the end of my vision for them. While my enthusiasm about serving them had never diminished, the church was at a crossroad and I did not know which way to lead them. Even though I prayed earnestly about their future, I could not get any sense of direction. It really came to a point of crisis for me personally because they were making decisions about which I had no confidence. As I prayed about it, I received a strong impression that it was time for me to move. In a matter of days, the Lord opened up a challenging opportunity to me. Every church needs a pastor who can serve with confidence and vision.

An inner restlessness may be a sign that you should move. We have to be careful at this point. Some persons seem to have been born restless. They have never learned the secrets of inner contentment. The grass always looks greener on the other side of the fence to them. This is not the type of restlessness I mean. This kind of restlessness needs to be solved with greater emotional maturity—not a new church. The inner restlessness that may be a sign comes to the heart of the pastor who is normally content. There is a mixture of discontent and anticipation in his heart. He senses that God is getting him ready for something new. While it is difficult to describe, it can be a part of the preparation of the Lord for a new challenge in his ministry. Such inner restlessness can be a sign that it is time to move.

The Lord may give you a heavenly mandate as a sign. This will be rare, but it does happen. After closing the door to which we have already referred in the life of Paul, He then opened one with a heavenly mandate. "During the night, Paul had a vision of a man of Macedonia standing and begging him, 'Come over to Macedonia and help us.' After Paul had seen the vision, we got ready at once to leave for Macedonia, concluding that God had called us to preach the gospel to them" (Acts 16:9-10, NIV). As far as I know, this only happened once in the life of Paul, but it did happen.

While I cannot lay claim to any such vision, I have experienced an overwhelming sense of divine leadership. When the search committee for the North Fort Worth Baptist church approached me, I had already determined in my mind that I was not interested. But while I was praying and reading in a hotel room in Dallas, Texas, on the afternoon that I was to meet with their committee, I received a compelling sense of call to that church. It came as I was reading about the experience of another pastor. What God had done in his life suddenly and unexpectedly became the divine direction for my life. It was the sign I needed to overcome my reluctance..

The ultimate thing you look for in deciding whether to go or to stay is the will of God. What is God's plan for your life? These signs may help you discern His will, but God is not limited. He can make His will known to you in a multitude of ways. The main thing for you is to make sure you are in a position to receive such insight from Him. He does make His will known to those who are ready to do His will in all things.

Changing churches is serious business for the pastor. Not only is his personal ministry and his family involved, but two congregations are also involved. If you are going to have a gracious end to your current ministry, you need to be able to approach it with the confidence that you are following the leadership of the Lord. You need the peace of God in your heart whether you go or whether you stay.

9
Openness
Sharing Your Heart

So you have decided that it is the will of God for you to move! What is the next step? You have already arranged a date with the new church for the presentation of your name. When do you tell the congregation you are currently serving about the decision? How do you let them know of the leadership of the Lord in your life? Because of the relationship that you have with them, they deserve to know of your decision very early. They deserve to hear about it from you. Openness and honesty with them is essential.

The Skepticism of the Laity

A time of pastoral change does not have to be a negative experience for the congregation. You must be prepared to do whatever you can to make it a positive experience. You should be aware that you will be facing a certain amount of skepticism among the laity about divine leadership in such decisions. This skepticism has been encouraged by things that have happened in the past.

The laity may be skeptical about your motives. They are confused when they hear the Lord given all of the credit for moves that obviously benefit the pastor in many ways. You may be moving to a larger church in a bigger city to receive a higher salary while living in a nicer house. The change will obviously put you in a position of greater influence in the denomination. They wonder if it requires much divine intervention to get you to do something so personally beneficial. They question among themselves why the Lord always seems to move men up the ladder of ministerial success. Does the Lord ever lead a man to a more difficult situation with a smaller salary? This is the kind of situation that your openness with them can help address.

As the pastor you can help the laity with this skepticism about motives. You can help them through your preaching and teaching ministry. A major objective for our preaching ministry must be to develop a way of looking at life from God's perspective. Is this not part of what it means to be godly? But it is even more important that we model such a life for them. If they have seen you approach all of your pastoral roles from such a perspective, they will understand your heart in such a big decision.

While sharing with the congregation, you should not try to appear super pious if the change in pastorates is to be profitable to you and your family. Neither should you be apologetic. The will of the Lord usually does involve moving men to places of larger responsibility. Maybe the corporate world learned from the Lord about testing men with smaller responsibilities before they placed them in larger responsibilities. At least we know that He was doing it long before it became a principle used by modern corporations. He allowed Joshua to work as the servant of Moses before He promoted him to the larger position. Jesus stated it well when He said, "Whoever is faithful in small matters will be faithful in large ones" (Luke 16:10, GNB). This could be one of the things you will want to share with your people. You can affirm the Lord's preparation in your life. I have always moved to a new pastorate with a sense that God had been preparing me for it. You can be open with them about your motives as you know them.

The laity may be skeptical about spiritual leadership. Pastors have spoken of divine leadership as though it were something unknown and strange to the person who sits in the pew. They cannot recall any such mystical experiences of divine leadership in their lives. If you will be open and honest with them about the experience, they will learn that it is not unlike things that have happened in their lives. You probably have not seen a vision, or heard a voice, or received any kind of mystical communication. Rather, several factors have combined to give you an inner sense of conviction that at this point in your life this is the right thing for you. The decision has not come without inner struggle. You may not have absolute certainty that this is the right thing, but you are stepping out in faith to do what you believe to be the will of God. Your testimony concerning divine leadership can encourage the laity to believe that they, too, can know the leadership of the Lord.

The Way to Openness

I learned to do this by a trial-and-error method. No one ever told me how to have a gracious ending to a pastorate. Because of my ignorance about how to do it, I did not do it very graciously at first. I treated the church as though I owed them no explanation. I related to them as though they were strangers—not as though they were actually my spiritual family. An inner desire to help them understand what was happening in my life prompted me to attempt openness with them.

It is better to share with your current church before you are called to the other congregation. Most congregations desire the prospective pastor to preach a trial sermon before they extend a call to him. You should be confident that you will accept their call, if it is extended, before you consent to preach before the church. When the decision is made to allow your name to be presented to the congregation, it is time to take your current church into your confidences. You can do this without making it a resignation. It is not appropriate to resign at this point. Rather, it is simply a testimony about your pilgrimage, about your desire to know the will of God, and a request for the understanding and prayers of your friends. They need to be aware that what now seems to be an open door may yet be shut by the Lord.

A Sunday evening worship service or a Wednesday night prayer meeting can be a good time for this sharing. It has been my practice to let this testimony be the sermon for the evening. It can surely qualify as a confessional type of sermon. The testimony should include only the positive things in the decision. This is not the time to take a cheap shot at some difficult people who have made the decision easier. While they may have made it easier to say yes, they should not be the primary motivation in the decision. Rather, you should focus on the positive signs that led you to this decision. You should affirm the congregation and express gratitude to them for their love and support.

When my family moved to the First Baptist Church, Lubbock, Texas, after some wonderful years of ministry with the First Baptist Church, Texarkana, Texas, I did this. After expressing to the congregation my desire to know the will of God and to do it, I told them about the First Baptist Church of Lubbock. I told them about some of the problems, the challenges, and the struggles of the Lubbock church. I told them about my prior experiences with the church when I had been a neighboring pastor in Lubbock. I shared with them my pilgrimage with the search committee. I shared with them the struggles I had been through in reaching a decision. I solicited their understanding and prayers for my family as we went to Lubbock to preach the next Sunday. It was a moving service for me and the church. It put our last days together into a special context. I sought to share with them as a friend to a friend. You can do this as you seek a gracious ending to your pastorate.

The Benefits of Openness

You will benefit from the openness. It will help you clarify your own feelings and motives. Each time I have done this, I have had a better understanding of my own decision. Verbalizing the decision helps clarify it.

Some parts of the experience cannot be put into words. You may have to confess, "I cannot give you a reason, but in my deepest heart I know that this is what God wants me to do." Your people will accept this. The people of the Lord know that the "ways of the Lord" are not our ways.

This openness will enhance the trust level in the congregation. Honesty and openness are essential elements in building trust. When such openness is not practiced, misunderstanding may develop and misinformation may be spread. Your openness will make it easier for the next pastor to have a healthy trust relationship with the congregation.

You need to anticipate that your leaving the church will trigger a grief process for both you and the congregation. Anger is a basic ingredient in the grief process. You may encounter some initial anger when you begin to share with the congregation your decision. Your openness will help prevent some of this anger. In its place, understanding and trust can be nurtured.

Your openness can be a model of a good approach to decision making for the laity. If you have gone about the decision in a mature way, the people can see how it is done. They will be able to appreciate the use of the Bible in seeking divine guidance. They will realize how important prayer is in such a process. They will have affirmed for them the importance of wise counsel. They will be reminded again of the importance of the will of God for all of life.

In my most recent experience of sharing such a decision with the congregation, a young graduate student was struggling with a career decision. After I had shared my pilgrimage in some detail, he came to me after the service to thank me. He had been greatly encouraged in his own search for the will of God in his life.

You have probably preached a sermon at some time on "Knowing the Will of God." Your testimony and openness will probably communicate more to them about knowing the will of God than your sermon ever did. Such a time of sharing is essential for a gracious ending.

10
Gratitude
Saying Your "Thank-You's"

One of the basic purposes of the last few days is to appropriately express your gratitude. No pastor, no matter how unpleasant his stay may have been, will be without some debts of gratitude to pay. When the decision for the move is made, some time should be spent making a complete list of those to whom you want to express gratitude. The family can be enlisted in this list-making task. If you have a secretary, she could probably be helpful.

Gratitude to Whom?

The persons on the list will vary from place to place, but you would probably want to include the following.

Staff

When the pastor leaves, staff members are affected more than anyone else. In many cases, they have been enlisted by you. They have been your loyal supporters through all kinds of experience. They have willingly overlooked your shortcomings. They have been willing to make you look good by their hard work. You have received the credit for much that they have achieved. Their names should be on your thank-you list.

Volunteer Leaders

Certain lay leaders have helped carry the burden. They may include the official lay leadership of the church, such as deacons, elders, stewards, committee chairpersons, Sunday School leaders, missions leaders, and others. Whatever has been accomplished during your years of ministry there, it would not have been possible without the support of the volunteer leadership of the church.

Support Groups

Your support group in a church may include persons who have not been in leadership positions. Yet, they have been persons who have provided encouragement at just the right time, who have given counsel when asked, and who have been a source of support. While your expression of gratitude to them may have to be more personal than public, it needs to be made.

New Members

There may be certain new members who have come into the congregation during your ministry to whom an expression of gratitude needs to be given. Their decision to become a part of the congregation may have been based on a personal friendship with you. Their commitment may have added strength to the life of the congregation. Again, the gratitude probably needs to be expressed in a personal way, but it should be made.

The Congregation

While the focus may need to be on key individuals or groups within the life of the church, the church itself must not be overlooked. We can follow the example of Paul in this. While he often attached special words of gratitude for individuals to his letters, he never forgot the congregation as a whole. His letters usually began with such an expression of gratitude to God for them. To the beloved Philippian church, he wrote, "I thank my God everytime I remember you" (Phil. 1:3, NIV). He even wrote to the troublesome Corinthian church, "I always thank God for you because of his grace given you in Christ Jesus" (I Cor. 1:4, NIV). We will do well to follow his example.

Community Friends

The life of the pastor in a community is never confined to his own congregation. He and his family develop ties with others in the community to whom some special gratitude needs to be expressed. They may include neighbors, doctors, teachers, a pharmacist, neighboring pastors, denominational officials, and servicemen. Many people make their contribution to our usefulness and happiness. As you are breaking ties with a community, do it gratefully.

How to Give Gratitude

There will be different ways to appropriately express gratitude with each group or person. You will have to consider in each case how it can best be done.

Gifts

A personal gift will be appropriate for certain key individuals. This will probably be reserved for those who have done more personal things for you. Your budget may put some limits on what you do, but even a small gift can say a big thank-you in such a setting.

Personal Notes

Just a little parting note that expresses gratitude will be meaningful. These will be especially meaningful if they are handwritten and reference is made to some specific instance of support or kindness. This will be better than just a regular thank-you note that you might purchase.

The Church Newsletter

The pastor's weekly column in the newsletter is usually well-read. It is a good place to say thank-you to the congregation and to certain program leaders, and staff leaders. You may even want to personalize it by listing names. All of us respond positively to such expressions of gratitude.

Letter to the Editor

Recently I read such a letter in our local newspaper. The departing pastor of a local congregation wrote a nice letter to the editor of the local paper. In the letter, he expressed gratitude to the members of his congregation and to certain persons in the community who had made his stay in the city a pleasant one. As I read the letter, I felt good about the man whom I only knew casually. It made me also feel good about his relationship with his congregation.

From the Pulpit

Verbal expressions of gratitude, when done in public, can be difficult. More than one pastor has been overcome by emotion as he tried to express gratitude before the congregation. These should probably be reserved for the congregation, the church leaders, workers in the Sunday School, and committees. Those that involve special helps from special individuals should be done more privately and personally.

Through Personal Contacts

These may include telephone calls to certain individuals. The calls may be brief, but may say much. Visitation time during the last days should be reserved as much as possible for such visits. Just to drop in on certain people and to say thank-you will mean much to them and enrich your own life.

Why Show Gratitude?

Why should we give so much attention to this? Would it not be easier to just ride off into the sunset and forget about these emotional encounters? It might be easier, but it would not be right.

We are under a biblical mandate to be grateful. When Paul admonished, "be ye thankful" (Col. 3:15), he surely included gratefulness in such relationships. While gratitude toward God is always imperative, it is also imperative to the willing vessels that God has used in ministering to us.

Since the pastor receives so much from so many, and is often treated as though he were a special person, he easily could begin to think that he deserves it. You may begin to accept such special treatment as a part of the compensation that goes with the calling. Paul not only admonish thankfulness but also practiced it. It would be helpful to do a personal study of the gratitude of Paul. You will find that this useful servant of God was always grateful for the least expression of support.

Such expressions of gratitude will also help the congregation. The resignation of a pastor will often evoke negative feelings in a congregation. They will begin to wonder if they have done something wrong. When I announced my intentions to resign to my first congregation, one of the older deacons asked, "Pastor, what is wrong? Has someone hurt your feelings?" His immediate thought was that something must be wrong or I would not have resigned. This is usually not the case. Usually when the pastor resigns, everything is right. Expressions of gratitude on the part of the pastor and his family will help the congregation feel this. It will protect the congregation from some of the misconceptions that they may have. It will help them know that you are not resigning because they have failed you in some way.

The pastor will also benefit. Something good happens in a person when he expresses gratitude. Some positive emotions are released that enrich life. Ending a good pastorate is not without pain. While saying thank-you will not prevent all of the pain, it will help.

A concern about first impressions is appropriate in most cases. Is not a concern about last impressions also appropriate? Would it not be good to be remembered as a thankful person? This might help them to forget some of your shortcomings that you hope they will forget.

11
Preparation
Making It Easy for Your Successor

When you have invested an extended period of your life in a ministry, you want to do all you can to preserve it. One thing the departing pastor can do to add grace to this departure is to assist the church in taking the necessary steps to find his replacement. Not everyone is agreed about what kind of role he should play during this time, but surely there is a role for him to play. He cannot end his concern for the welfare of the church by simply reading a statement of resignation.

Through Preaching

The pastor will usually have from two to four weeks to preach to the congregation after his resignation. While he will sense a definite difference in his relationship with the people, he must still make the most of the opportunity. God is still pleased to use preaching to meet the needs of His people.

This is not a time to use the pulpit to solve problems you have not been able to solve during your pastorate, though it can be tempting. You will be tempted to address courageously some situation that you did not have the courage to address before. One young pastor wanted to use his remaining days with the congregation to outline a plan for their future. It was a plan that he had not been able to share with them during his years of pastorate. Some deacons counseled him wisely to leave such things in the hands of his successor. It was too late for that type of preaching. The pastor should resist the temptation to use the pulpit in those closing days in this way.

Rather, it is a time to preach on themes that encourage prayer, faith, and confidence. The attention of the congregation needs to be focused on the unchanging God. The change of leaders in the work of the Lord does not reflect a change in God. They need to be reminded that God's purpose for His church does not change. They need to be reminded that the church can find the will of God for its future through prayer.

After resigning from one pastorate, I found encouragement for myself and the people by preaching from the letters to the churches in Revelation. However, instead of focusing on the problems which the Lord addressed in the churches, I preached on the manner in which Jesus revealed Himself to the churches. The problems do not look impossible when you look at them in the light of who He is. I preached on the promises the Lord gave to the churches. These promises will bring confidence and hope to any congregation.

Such preaching will make the pastor more than a lame duck. It will bring some special excitement to the worship experiences. They can often become the most fruitful days of a person's ministry in a church.

Through His Leadership

Although the pastor's leadership role is altered by his resignation, some tasks still need to be done by the outgoing pastor. He should try to accomplish at least four things before he moves.

First, he should lead the church to get a pastor search committee elected. The church may have an established procedure by which this is accomplished. If the church has adopted by-laws, this is probably spelled out in them. If there are no written by-laws, a tradition may have the same authority. The manner in which the committee is selected is not important if the church is comfortable with it. The committee does need to have the confidence and the support of the church. The pastor's task is simply to see that this is accomplished. He will have to give encouragement to the appropriate people who have assignments in the process.

In some cases, the process may require more time than the pastor has available. Even then, he can at least meet with and give encouragement to those who are in places of responsibility. If he has had a long pastorate, the process may be new to those who are in leadership positions. The pastor's encouragement will be helpful to them.

He should assist in getting a pulpit committee trained. Once the committee is selected, they need training. Their task is too important for them to attempt it without proper training. If the committee is willing, the pastor can fill this role. If the committee is not willing, he can at least point them to someone who can provide good training. In most cases, the area denominational leadership, such as a Baptist director of missions, is equipped for this task. He can save the committee many unnecessary miles and disappointments if they will spend some time with him.

The committee needs to be equipped spiritually. They need to be instructed in the importance of prayer in discovering the will of God. They need to be instructed in the importance of their relationship with each other. They must move to a deeper level of brotherly love than they have ever known before. A wise pastor can help them with this.

The committee needs to be equipped for their task. In many cases they will be confronted with a large stack of recommendations. Some of the recommendations will claim to be the expression of a special revelation from the Lord. How could the one Lord guide several persons to give a committee conflicting advice? Not every committee member is ready for this kind of experience. You can help the members understand that not everyone who claims to have heard from the Lord actually heard Him. They also need to know that usually the Lord chooses to speak personally to committee members and not through some unknown person.

They will need your counsel in how to respond to recommendations. They need a plan that will save them precious time and energy. They need a plan for quickly eliminating those who are not valid prospects. They need help in knowing who is a prospect. You are the person in the best position to provide this help.

The committee needs guidance in establishing the procedures they will follow. Will they seek input from the congregation? Will they operate confidentially? Will they always travel together? Will they have a conference with each person they hear? Will they let the prospective pastor know that they will be in the worship service? Without some well-conceived plans a committee can waste a lot of time and money. I remember a committee from a large church who came to hear me preach. They traveled a long way at a considerable expense only to hear me read my resignation. I had just accepted another church. They did not have a good plan of operation. While the pastor cannot give them a plan to follow, he can at least point them in the right direction.

He should assist in getting the question of an interim pastor settled. Who will preach the Sunday after you are gone? While this is not your responsibility, you should help those who are responsible. The church may be guided by their by-laws in this matter also. Some churches have a standing pulpit supply committee who becomes responsible. Some churches make this the first task of the pulpit search committee. They are to bring to the church a recommendation concerning an interim pastor as soon as possible. Some churches have a tradition that they have followed. The pastor should again give encouragement to those who are responsible.

The question of an interim pastor is one to be settled by the congregation. If there is a godly person available who is not a prospective pastor for the church, the church is usually best served by an interim pastor. A retired minister, a college or seminary professor, a denominational worker, or a furloughing missionary can usually be found. He will provide the church with stability and wise counsel through this testing time. You may want to provide them with a list of persons to consider. If it is the practice of the church to use supply preachers, you may want to help them put together such a list of prospects. You will be in a better position than the committee members to know persons who can preach.

The pastor should assist in getting the organizational leadership in place for the interim. The church must continue to minister without a pastor. If there is a staff, their role during this period must be determined. In some cases, the church by-laws will designate one of the staff members as the staff and program leader during the interim. If this is not set forth in the by-laws of the church, you should help the church in designating a staff leader. If there is a multiple staff, such a designation of a leader is important. You may want to lead the lay leadership of the church to give some encouragement to the staff. They may feel threatened when the pastor resigns. Are they expected to resign, too, even if they have no place to go? Should they begin looking for another place to serve? These are difficult times for them. They need to have their ministry position made as secure as possible for the health of the church during this period.

If there is no professional staff, you need to meet with the lay leadership. They need to be aware of their increased responsibility during this time. The chairman of the deacons, the Sunday School leaders, the Church Training leaders, the missions leaders, the music leaders, and the finance leaders need a word of encouragement from you. They need to know that their steadfastness in their task will give assurance to the congregation. While they are not called to replace the pastor in the life of the church, they do carry an extra load.

If you have accomplished these four tasks, you will add grace to the end of your ministry.

Through Counsel

How much counsel should you give? Should you recommend persons to be considered as your successor? You will have to answer this question for yourself. I have always refrained from doing this. My primary reason for refraining from such recommendations is that I would tend to recommend someone whose style of ministry is much like mine. The Lord may want to do something different through the next person. I am willing to trust the committee to the wise hands of the Lord.

What I have offered the committee is my counsel. I have offered to respond to any question that they might present to me concerning any person they are considering. I believe I have been helpful to committees in this way. I also have invited them to invite any person they are considering to call me. I will be happy to give them my candid appraisal of the church. I believe that I have been helpful in this way, also.

You can also point the church and the committee toward wise counsel. They will find the leader in their local denominational unit to be a wise counselor. They will find the staff of the state or regional denominational unit to be ready to assist. Most denominations have a designated person with the assignment of providing assistance to committees.

Wise counsel can save a church some bad experiences. One church discovered that their new pastor had serious financial and moral problems. The problems were not new. If the committee had sought some wise counsel from denominational leadership, they could have informed them of the man's problems.

You can also provide the committee with some good resource material. Rather than indicating that such material is available, you should be bold enough to purchase it for them. You might even want to make it a personal gift to the committee. Good resource materials are available at Baptist Book Stores. You can keep the committee from approaching the task as if they were the first search committee to ever be formed.

This is a vital part of a gracious ending. If you can leave the church equipped to prayerfully find your successor, you have done much to preserve the investment you have made in the life of the church.

12
Business
Leave Your House in Order

Just being a good Christian will help you have a gracious ending. If you will simply apply the Golden Rule to this situation, you will have a good conclusion to your work. You should do the things for your successor and for the church that you would expect if you were the new pastor. This is particularly true in your business affairs.

Debts

You should pay all of your debts or make arrangements for them before you leave. Pastors do not always live within their incomes. They sometimes borrow money or buy things on credit from local merchants. More than one pastor has been known to leave town with unpaid debts. One pastor had borrowed money from several members of the church. Each person had loaned him money without knowing that he was also borrowing from others. It was not until he left town without paying any of them that the truth began to come out. Can you imagine the distrust that the new pastor had to face when he was called to the church?

What may be even worse is the pastor who bought things on credit from several local merchants and left town without paying. In this case, the new pastor had to face a compromised witness in the community as well as distrust in the church. It can take a decade of good living and ministry to overcome such a failure. Your practicing the Golden Rule will keep this from happening.

If you have financial problems, you will want to work out a plan for solving them before you make the pastoral change. If local debts are involved, you may want to consolidate them into one note at the local bank before you move. If this is not possible, you should personally visit with each local creditor and assure him of your intentions to take care of your debts as soon as possible. You will ensure your successor against a climate of distrust. You will want this part of your house in order before you make the change.

Leave Helpful Things

You should leave behind everything that will be helpful to the new pastor. This will require some thought on your part. Why not make a list of things that you would appreciate finding if you were to be the new pastor? You will probably come up with a rather lengthy list.

Plans

Has the church built a new building during your pastorate? The plans for the new building do not belong to you, unless you drew them. While it may be fine to carry a copy of the plans with you, you will want to make sure that a full set of the plans is left behind for the pastor and the church. There will be many occasions when they will be useful.

Has the church developed some plans for buildings that have not yet been built? These, too, belong to the church, whether the church has adopted them or not. The church paid for them. Even though the church may never adopt them, they will be helpful in acquainting the new pastor with the things that have been considered in the past. Make sure that the plans are left in a place where the new pastor can find and use them.

Goals

If the church has adopted some long-range goals and plans, a copy of these should be left in the pastor's desk. He should not have to search a week to find a copy. Whether the goals are to be pursued or not, they will be helpful to the new pastor in understanding where the church has been and where it is going.

Prospect Lists

If you have a personal prospect list from which you have been working, leave it for the new pastor. It may ensure that the seed you have sown will be harvested. You might even want to leave a list with some helpful information about each person or family. He could profit from what you have learned about certain unsaved and unchurched prospects.

If there is a church prospect file, leave it for the pastor. Do not take it with you or destroy it. Such a list can save the pastor months of time and make his beginning with the church more fruitful.

Instructions

Did you receive instruction manuals with the equipment that is used in the office or the church? Make sure that you leave these in a handy place for the new pastor. You may have known the frustration of searching for that service manual that went with the copy machine! Remember the Golden Rule!

Papers

You may have folders of materials in your files that the new pastor would find beneficial. Go through your files with him in mind. If you think it would be helpful to him, leave it behind. If you want to keep it, at least make him a copy. When in doubt about its usefulness, leave it for him. He would rather throw away something that was not helpful than not have a useful piece of material.

Keys

A set of keys to everything, placed in the desk drawer, or left with a church leader, with each labeled, is a gracious gift. It could be one of the more practical things that you can do for your successor. The keys do go with the job!

Cards

Since we live in the day of the plastic card, make sure that you leave those that the new pastor will need. This would include any credit cards that the church has provided for you—such as gasoline or telephone. If the local hospital has issued you a card that gives entrance to the parking lot, you will want to include it.

Telephone Lists

You will want to leave an up-to-date church directory, plus a list of telephone numbers that he may need in the early days of his work. This will be especially important if there is no secretary to help him find his way around. Remember the Golden Rule should be your guide in making this list of things to leave.

Things that Belong to the Church

You should leave behind everything that belongs to the church. Maybe we should underline the word *everything*. If you have served the church for a number of years, the question of ownership may get clouded. Using a thing for ten years does not make you the owner of it if you did not buy it or it was not given to you. You will want this part of your house to be in order.

Furniture

This includes file cabinets, chairs, desks, typewriters, shelves, telephones, and anything else that may furnish your office or parsonage. If you are in doubt about the ownership, ask. Some member may have given a piece of furniture for your office, but, in his understanding, he did not give it to you personally. It was for your use, but the church is the owner. If you take it with you, you will be remembered as a thief. It is better to leave something behind that actually belongs to you than to take something that belonged to the church.

Books

It is easy for a book from the church library to find its way into the pastor's library. He can become a thief without ever intending it. A careful survey of your library before moving can solve this problem. You may also find books or articles that have been borrowed from members of the congregation or neighboring ministers that you will want to return. Attention to the little things is a part of having your house in order.

Equipment

Churches are generous in providing us with equipment to use in our ministry. When you have used it regularly for an extended period of time, you may actually feel that it is yours. It may be so much a part of you that you will want to purchase it from the church before you leave. However, when the van pulls out, it should not have anything on it that belongs to the church. Not even a pencil!

Money

You may have some money that belongs to the church. Many churches have a plan to help their pastor purchase a home. They may make him an interest-free loan that is to be returned when he sells his house. They may have some other kind of arrangement with you. If you are a party to any such generous arrangement, make sure that you handle it in a businesslike way. Their generosity with the next pastor will be affected by how you handle it.

My wife has a distressing compulsion—at least it is distressing to me. Whenever we move, she wants to do everything possible to make it easy for the people who will buy our house. She knows that the condition in which they find the house will be a reflection on her. So when we are trying to get out of town, there is always one last thing that needs to be done. Her dedication to this has been know to delay our departure for hours. This can be hard on a husband's patience. My inclination is to let the buyer worry about all of these little things, but every departing pastor need this same type of compulsion about leaving his house in order. It will add grace to his departure, and a blessing to his successor. It is part of a gracious ending.

13
Ethics
Relating to Your Successor in a Christian Way

The Golden Rule is your guide. How you relate to your successor should be guided by how you will want your predecessor to relate to you. Anyone who has observed the dynamics of a good beginning knows that your predecessor can make a difference. So you can make a difference for your successor. Being committed to this for good is a part of a gracious ending. It is another way of preserving the investment that you have made in the church. Much has been written on this aspect of the pastoral ministry. Let us consider some things that will help.

Prayer

You should pray for him. I learned this from the apostle Paul. Several years ago, I was impressed with the way Paul prayed for the churches he had once served. "I thank my God upon every remembrance of you, Always in every prayer of mine for you all making request with joy" (Phil. 1:3-4). This word to the Philippians is typical. While Paul did not specifically pray for the pastor in Philippi, surely he did not overlook the person most responsible for their spiritual welfare. Since I learned this, I have made it a practice to thank God weekly for the churches that I have served and to pray for their present pastors. This has brought great joy to my life and made it possible for me to rejoice in every victory the new pastor experiences. I have had a part in the victories through my work there and through my continuing prayer. This will bless you and your successor.

Counsel

You should offer counsel only when it is sought. Your successor may not seek it. If he does not, do not give it. It would be appropriate to write a letter or make a personal call to him once he has been called to the church. You can assure him of your prayers and offer your assistance. From that point, the initiative should be with him. He needs the freedom to lead the church under the lordship of Christ. If you had been essential for the progress of the church, the Lord would have left you there.

Affirmation

You should always affirm the new pastor's ministry. In most cases, you will continue to have contact with members of the church. They will have reports to share of the work of the new pastor. They will watch your reaction. When you speak of his ministry, you should speak affirmatively. A negative comment from you could encourage disloyalty or could sow a seed of doubt.

He will probably do things differently. Pastors have been gifted by God in different ways. You need to be big enough to see the work of God being done uniquely through him. The pastor of a local church has enough problems without the former pastor viewing his work through critical eyes. You will be helped by remembering the attitude of Paul toward those in Rome with whom he had some differences. He rejoiced in the gospel that was preached through them (Phil. 1:18).

Freedom

You should allow him to do the things that will enhance his ministry. If you had a good ministry in the church, and you are not moving too far away, some people will turn to you in their times of crises. It is the opportunity to minister to people in these special times that builds a base for ministry in a congregation. If you take these away from the new pastor, you will limit his ability to become the pastor.

In most cases, you should allow him to do the weddings. There may be a rare exception, but, even then, you should make sure that it is done with his blessing. You should send the couple desiring your services to him to explain why they are asking you or you should call him yourself. It should never be a surprise to him. In most cases, you will be able to gracefully encourage the couple to allow the new pastor to perform the wedding. They probably have not considered how important this ministry is to him.

In most cases, you should allow him to do the funerals. If you made a promise to someone that you would do his or her funeral, it may be permissible to return. In most cases, it would be better to excuse yourself or to offer to assist as the pastor does the funeral. In the cases in which I have gone back to do a funeral, I have been painfully aware that I was able to give to them only a partial pastoral ministry. You are not in a position to be their counselor and supporter in the difficult days that are ahead.

The same is true of special events. If you are invited back to participate in some special event, it should always be with the pastor's blessing. In every way possible, you should do what you can to enhance his position as the pastor of the church.

There will be some members in every congregation who are about two pastors behind in their loyalty. You should not feel overly complimented when some of them develop a strong case of loyalty toward you when you become their former pastor. I have observed that the more mature members of the church will open their hearts to their new shepherd. This will especially be true if their former shepherd indicates that this is the proper thing to do.

Friendships

You should be careful of friendships with members of the congregation. There is nothing wrong with developing friendships with the people you serve. There would be something artificial about your approach to ministry if this did not happen. Relating to these friends when you become their former pastor can be a problem. Is it necessary to end such friendships? I do not think so. It simply means that you have to handle these friendships wisely. You must guard against continuing in the pastoral role with these persons. The friendship should never be a cause of distress to the present pastor. He should feel sure that you are his supporter in his work with the church. If he is threatened by your continued friendship with the individuals, you should be willing to terminate the friendship. However, you must be careful to do this in a way that will not place blame on the pastor. The friend should probably never know the reason that it became necessary for you to withdraw from the close relationship. You will add grace to the ending of your ministry in this church if you are willing to pay this kind of price for the success of your successor.

Staff

You should be careful about approaching staff members to join your church. This confronts us with a thorny problem. Are you free to invite members of the staff to join you in your new church? How you answer this question may be influenced by your view of the staff. Are they your staff? Or are they the ministerial staff of the church? My own view is that they are the ministerial staff of the church. They are God-called servants of the church of Jesus Christ. I have had the privilege of working with them as a fellow minister. A part of my responsibility has been to function as the God-appointed leader of the staff and congregation. I am afraid that staff relations in the modern church may be more influenced by the world of business than by the New Testament.

However, this does not mean that special relationships may not develop between a pastor and a particular staff member. The relationship may be such a happy one that they feel compelled to maintain it in another church. How do you go about this without doing harm to your former church?

You must honestly face the question of what is best for the former church. Will it do them harm if you invite the staff member to leave now? Surely the Lord would not harm them in order to bless you. There are times when it may well be in the best interest of everyone concerned for the staff person to move now. If, after prayerful consideration, you feel this to be true, then proceed.

If the church has not called a pastor yet, you should contact key leaders of the church to explain your actions. They should know your heart. They should know your reasoning. They should know that it is not your desire to do them harm. They should know of your continued concern for the church. If the church has called a new pastor, you should approach him before approaching the staff member. He, too, should know of your concern for him and the success of his work. In most cases, you will be able to proceed with his full blessing. He may even prefer to have the privilege of leading the church to enlist someone to fill such a position who is more attuned to his approach to ministry and personality.

Your goal must always be to do that which will enhance the work of the new pastor.

Helper

You should cultivate the new pastor's friendship. Who could not use one more good friend? If the distance is such that you can expect to have fairly frequent contact with the new pastor, work on being his friend. If he has moved to an area where he does not have many friends, he may welcome this.

Our churches would be encouraged if they could see more brotherly conduct and attitudes among those in the ministry. Too many times we have related to each other like representatives of competing companies rather than servants of the same Lord and brothers in the same family.

In summary, the Golden Rule can be your guide. It will be better than any set of rules that we might put together. Since it is a practical way of putting love into action, it can be applied to any situation. You will never go wrong if you use it as your guide. Both you and the person who follows you will experience grace. It will enhance a graceful ending to a good thing!

14
The Parting
What the Church Can Do

The church can do some things to make the ending gracious. As the pastor, you may want to drop some hints in this direction even though most of them will be for your benefit. While they will benefit you as the pastor, they will be healthy for the church and will protect the church from bad attitudes at this time. The leaving of a pastor is always a time of testing for the church.

Write a Note

Written expressions of gratitude to the pastor and his family can be very meaningful. Such notes can be kept for encouragement during some difficult times. It is just a little gesture on the part of church members, but collectively it becomes a large expression of gratitude.

When my family moved from one pastorate, the hospitality committee had made a large mailbox which they placed in a prominent place at the reception they had for us. As the members went through the line, they dropped their personal notes into the mailbox. Some were meaningful cards while others were personal letters. Our family had some uplifting times as we read them one by one. It helped us leave with a warm glow in our hearts.

A Reception

A reception has become traditional for the departing pastor. It can be very meaningful for the pastor's family, as well as the church family. In a larger congregation, there will be some people with whom you will not have an opportunity to visit without a reception.

Plans for the reception should be developed and carried out by the appropriate committee in the church. The committee will want to schedule the reception at a time that will be convenient for the people. They will want to schedule it at a time when it will not be hurried. Special invitations should be sent to others in the community who might want to be a part of honoring the pastor and his family. The committee may want to prepare a display of pictures and other things that will reflect the ministry of the pastor with the church.

The reception is probably not the best place for public expressions of appreciation for the pastor or speeches to be made. These should be given in one of the regular times of worship where the whole congregation can participate. Rather, the reception should be a time for personal contact with the larger body of the church as they personally express their words of appreciation to the pastor and his family.

Such a reception will require preparation and work, but it is worth it. It will be a gift that the pastor's family will always carry with them in their memory.

Honor Commitments

The resignation of a beloved pastor can provoke some bad feelings. The church may feel like they have been betrayed or forsaken. They may even be tempted to draw back from some commitments they have made to the pastor. If the pastor has vacation time coming, they should see that it is given to him. If there is some other salary consideration that he is due, it should be given to him. The rule for the church should be generosity. Even if the pastor is going to a larger church for a higher salary, his move will be costly to him personally.

Even though it is not a commitment, there is one other thing that the church can do that will be helpful. The church should make sure that the pastor's family has health insurance until they are able to be covered by their new church. Three friends of mine have been involved in tragic car accidents while in the process of moving from one place of service to another. Without the generosity of the churches they were leaving, they would have been financially ruined.

The leaders of the church must be sensitive. Sometimes a bitter person will surface during such a time and will oppose any generosity toward the pastor. He or she will seize it as a last opportunity to hurt the pastor. Such an immature attitude must not be the memory that the pastor carries away with him. Rather, he and his family should go away with a just reason to thank God for the kindness and generosity of His people. The elected leaders of the church must be ready to give wise guidance to the church at such a time. The pastor should not be put in a position where he has to ask for these things.

Pray

Studies about the causes of stress put making such a move high on their list. They put it right under death in the family or other such traumatic experiences. This means that the pastor and his family will be under great stress as they finish their work with your church and begin their move to the new church. Stress can be dangerous to the health of the persons involved, as well as difficult for the relationships within the family.

Every pastor needs the prayers of the people who love him

in such a time. While he has been called to a new church, the present congregation will have a greater love for him and a deeper understanding of his needs. Earnest intercessory prayer for the pastor and each member of his family will bring divine resources to them in their time of need. The children of the family especially should be included in the prayers. They have to go through all of the trauma of the move with the pastor without fully sharing in his sense of call. They leave behind some very close friends and an important support system. They will be going to a new school where they will feel like strangers. You can pray that God will help them during this adjustment period.

What do you pray for as you intercede for the pastor and his family? You can pray that God will protect them from physical harm as they move. You can pray that God will keep them in health. You can pray that God will guide them to the right house and help them sell their present home. This is always a source of anxiety if they own their home. You can pray that the Lord will give them favor among the new congregation. You can pray that the Lord's peace will be upon the family through the whole process. You can pray that the Lord will give them supporting friends in their new location—especially the wife and children. You might even want to ask the pastor if there are other needs for which you could pray.

Your prayers are a precious parting gift to your pastor. They will help him have a gracious ending.

A Task Force

Thank God for the Marthas of the congregation! This is that company of persons to whom God has given a serving spirit. They usually have the beautiful gift of helps. Such a gift can be very helpful to the pastor's family as they move. Moving is just plain hard work! Even though you use professional movers, it is still hard work. Just a few willing hands can make the task a whole lot easier.

It is good to keep in mind that the pastor's family is usually emotionally and physically exhausted as they come to the moving time. The last few days with the church will be filled with a round of meetings that will take up every spare moment. Then moving day comes. The pastor's wife will wonder, *Will I make it?* Sure she can, if someone will take care of her children while she is packing and cleaning. She can if another person will run errands for her. She can if another friend will be available to assist with the last minute emergencies. She can if someone else will make sure she does not have to cook on moving day.

These are the kinds of things love is made of. If there have been helping hands, you will go away knowing that you were loved.

A Gift

Should the church give the pastor and his family a gift? Probably. There may be special circumstances in which a gift would not be appropriate, but in most cases it would be appropriate. The nature of the gift would be determined by the circumstances. The length of the pastor's work with the church should be taken into consideration. Special needs that may be a part of the pastor's family should also be considered. It is probably not appropriate to give a young pastor and his family a silver service if they really need a bed for the new baby. It is amazing how basic and practical the young pastor and his wife can be in their thinking! Above all, the gift should express the love and appreciation of the people.

Such a gift can be given at the reception, but it may be more appropriate to present it in a worship service. Usually more people will have the joy of being a part of the presentation if it is given in the worship service.

The Parting

I have put the burden for a gracious ending on the pastor in this book. This is the way it should be. In most cases, the ending of the pastorate is the pastor's decision. He is the leader of the congregation. His attitude and actions will determine what happens. But there are these things, and more, that a congregation can do to add some grace to the ending.

Grace is the key word. The pastor does not assume that the church owes him anything. He thanks God for the gracious gift of allowing him to serve the church. But grace and kindness on the part of the church will make a difficult experience easier for the pastor's family.

Appendix

Figure 1
Check List for Clarity in a Call

	YES	NO
1. Church moves/provides moving expenses?	___	___
2. Church provides housing for pastor, family?	___	___
If yes, in what form?		
Pastorium ___		
Allowance ___		
If allowance, how much monthly? ___		
3. Church provides utilities or allowance? If yes, amount:	___	___
Electricity $ ___		
Phone $ ___		
Water $ ___		
Other $ ___		
4. Church assists pastor in purchasing home?	___	___
If yes, indicate the following: Provides down payment as gift or loan in the amount of $ ___ at an interest rate of ___ % to be repaid at $ ___ monthly. Amount to be paid in full within ___ days of termination as pastor.		
5. Monthly salary to begin $ ___ with review for increase at the end of: ___ Months ___ (How often?) Year ___	___	___
Recommendation for increase to be made by ___ committee.		
6. Monthly car allowance provided?	___	___
If yes, in the amount of $ ___ per month and ___ ¢ per mile for distant travel on church business.		
7. Church provides insurance coverage? If yes, how much?	___	___
Health $ ___		
Life $ ___		
Retirement $ ___		
8. Church provides annual book allowance?	___	___
If yes, annual amount $ ___		

9. Church provides weekly days off? _____
   If yes, number of days _____
10. Church provides annual, paid vacation? _____
   If yes, number of weeks _____ first year; second year _____ and thereafter _____
11. Is pulpit supply paid by church for vacation absences? _____
12. Church provides time off for:
   Revivals? _____
   State Convention? _____
   Southern Baptist Convention? _____
   How much time for revivals? _____
13. Is pulpit supply paid by church for these absences? _____
14. Are expenses paid to conventions? _____
   Wife included? _____
15. Church provides time off for bereavement? _____
   If yes, how much time? _____
16. Church provides time off for illness? _____
   If yes, amount of time annually _____
17. Are salary and benefits paid during time of illness? _____
   For how long? _____
18. Supply minister paid by church? _____
   For how long? _____
19. Church provides annual physical examination for pastor? _____
20. Pastor is designated as supervisor of other staff? _____
   If no, who is designated and for which staff members? _____
21. Time off is provided for study leave and training conferences? _____
   If yes, how much time annually? _____
22. Does church pay cost of job-related training? _____
   If yes, how much of total cost? _____
23. _____
24. _____
25. _____

Figure 2

Specific Agreements (These Will Vary from Church to Church)

Annual Financial Arrangements

1. VOCATIONAL COMPENSATION
   Base Salary: to be paid .... $ _____

   Housing   Parsonage
   Allowance _____ Rental Value _____

   Utilities   Utilities
   Allowance _____ Estimate _____
                              TOTAL $ _____

2. FRINGE BENEFITS
   Retirement Plans: _____ % of
     Vocational Compensation $ _____
   Family Health Insurance:
     _____ Pastor's Part _____ All
   Life Insurance on Pastor _____
   Disability Insurance on Pastor _____
   Tax Deferred Annuity _____
                           TOTAL $ _____

Annual Time Arrangements

The church acknowledges that the pastor's work cannot be rigidly regulated because of the nature of ministry. Crisis situations and emergencies along with meetings and a heavy schedule may alter the pastor's schedule and sometimes necessitate his arranging his work and leisure at his own convenience. Despite week-end work and evening obligations, the pastor must find some time to spend with his family and for his own personal needs.

1. Day(s) a week off _____
2. Weeks for vacation _____
3. List holidays _____
4. Study leave time _____
5. Revivals or Sunday engagements _____

3. PROFESSIONAL EXPENSES
   Car Allowance: to be paid _____ $ _____
   *Conventions and Meetings _____
   Book Allowance _____
                              TOTAL $ _____

4. NECESSARY EXPENDITURES
   Social Security Tax Allowance:
   _____ Half _____ All $ _____
   Workman's Compensation _____
                              TOTAL $ _____

5. ANY OTHER CONSIDERATIONS
   Christmas Bonus or Cash Gift $ _____
   Homeowners Insurance on
   Parsonage _____
                              TOTAL $ _____

6. Total number of Sundays for
   church-paid pulpit supplies _____
   Vacation time _____
   Conventions or conferences _____
   Study leave _____
   Revivals and engagements _____

7. Sick leave arrangements: _____

8. Any other arrangements: _____

*Professional Expenses, Conventions and Meetings

_____ For expenses at meeting attended as pastor
_____ Includes pastor's spouse when she accompanies
_____ For study leave and continuing education
_____ For civic club membership expenses
_____ To be used at pastor's discretion
_____ Pastor to give account for reimbursement
_____ Surplus belongs to _____ pastor _____ church

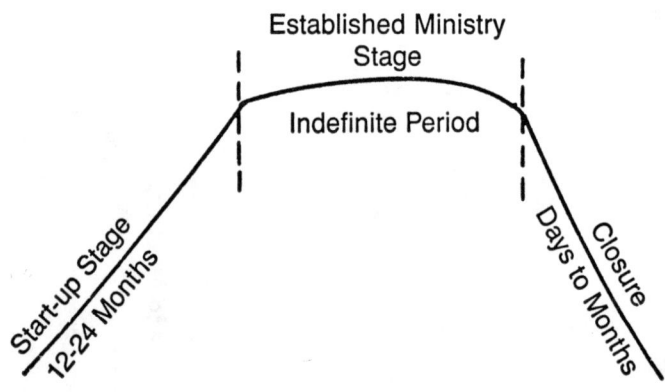

Figure 3

Note: Figures 1, 2, and 3 are from Bruce Powers, ed., *Church Administration Handbook* (Nashville: Broadman Press, 1985), pp. 278-279, 280-281, 310.

Notes